Au Revoir, Sarnia Chérie

Good-bye, Dear Guernsey

A personal account of the idyllic life a boy and his family enjoyed in Guernsey until, on 19th June 1940, their life—and that of all Channel Islanders—was rudely disrupted.

Ron Blicq

RGI International

Other Publications by Ron Blicq

Education

Books

Get to the Point! *
Technically-Write! *
Administratively-Write!
Communicating at Work
Guidelines for Report Writing *
Writing Reports to Get Results *

* *Co-authored with Lisa Moretto*

Videoscripts

Go For It!
6 Around a Table
Sell Yourself Well
Scaling the Pyramid
So, You Have to Give a Talk?
Sharpening Your Communication Skills

Drama

Chords, Accords and Discords
The Railway Children
The Lollystick Wand

Au Revoir, Sarnia Chérie

This book is dedicated to:

All those parents in the Channel Islands who, on 19th June 1940, had to decide almost at a moment's notice whether to send their children to Britain with the school they were attending, or to keep them at home to live under enemy occupation. Almost all gave approval for their children to be evacuated. Many did not see their children again for five long years.

All the children who were evacuated.

All their teachers, who not only acted as teachers but also became their mentors, friends and, in many cases, the equivalent of substitute parents.

First published in Canada in 2000
RGI International Inc, 569 Oxford Street, Winnipeg MB
www.rgilearning.com

The moral right of the author has been asserted
A CIP catalogue record of this book is available from
National Library of Canada

ISBN 0-9686989-0-5

Printed and bound by PeterPrint
Guernsey, C.I.

6 5 4 3 2

Cover design and illustrations by Carol Kemp
Photographs on p 10, 26, 65, 80 by Carel Toms

The incidents in this book are true, although in some cases a person's name has been changed to protect the individual's identity

Contents

Acknowledgments

I particularly appreciated the advice and encouragement I received from Lisa Moretto, who reviewed the first version of the manuscript; from Carel Toms, who searched for the photographs; and from Carol Kemp, who intuitively illustrated the book for me.

Foreword

I am an expatriate Guernseyman now living on the plains of Western Canada. (Can you imagine trading the cliffs and beaches, rolling countryside and winding lanes of Guernsey for miles and miles of absolutely flat fields of waving wheat and rapeseed punctuated every mile by an absolutely straight road that disappears over the horizon?) So every year or two I "fly home" to recharge my personal batteries.

During my visits to Guernsey over the years I have noticed a proliferation of books about the island in general and the occupation in particular. But I have seen very little written about the evacuation that preceded the occupation, and how it felt to be one of the children who were evacuated. Molly Bihet has done an excellent job in documenting her experience as a child who remained here during the occupation. In these pages I will throw a little light on those momentous hours in the latter half of June 1940 that disrupted the home life of so many of the island's children, and concurrently ended for ever my family's equable lifestyle in Guernsey.

So prepare to meet my family and experience some of the pleasures of living on this jewel of an island in the 1920s and 1930s. Then see through a boy's eyes what it was like to be suddenly and unexpectedly uprooted and sent to an unknown shore. And perhaps understand why I am continually being drawn back to Guernsey, the island of my birth.

A Note on The Book Title

Sarnia is the Norman name for Guernsey. The expression "Sarnia Chérie" is drawn from a patois song about the singer's love for the Island.

Part 1

Unexpected News
June 1940

1

An Early Morning Telephone Call

I was wakened by a shout from Ian, my youngest brother, in the next room.

'The telephone's ringing! Daddy! The telephone!'

Only then did I hear the muffled but insistent jangling from the wood-encased instrument mounted high on the wall in the dining room, behind the door to the kitchen. The operator must have been trying to raise an answer for some time, for the rings had become long, drawn-out, persistent.

I sensed rather than heard my father's bare feet padding through the living room. But his exasperated '*All right!*' was unmistakeable (although I couldn't be sure whether he was answering Ian's insistent call or mumbling an unheard protest to the operator). Then the ringing stopped, interrupted by a shouted 'Hullo?' and indistinct, monosyllabic responses that lasted for some seven or eight minutes. I wondered if my father was being given an advance warning of an air raid, or news of an invasion attempt, and I checked in the half-light that my gas mask and helmet were beside my desk. The hands on my Big Ben pointed to 17 minutes past 6. It would be another hour and a quarter before the alarm was set to jangle me into wakefulness at 7:30.

I reached above my head with one hand and felt

along the top of the headboard until my fingers curled around a slim cord that dangled from the ceiling. It was connected, through a series of pulleys I had screwed into the picture rail, to the curtains above the double window on the far side of the room.

As I tugged on the cord the thick blackout curtains pulled apart in a series of jerks, flooding the bedroom with light and revealing clusters of pink roses growing in profusion over the arched entrance to the front garden. Bees were already busy in the early morning sunlight, buzzing from one set of dew-rimmed petals to the next, their legs busily thrusting pollen into the sacks in their abdomens.

I pulled on my dressing gown and paused beside my two-seat school desk to change the date on my calendar. Spreading the ivory cubes on their backward-sloping base, I lifted out one with a black '8' etched into its face, turned it until the '9' faced me, inserted the cube into the open space, and pressed the five cubes together between my outstretched thumb and forefinger until they read: 19 6 40: 19th June 1940. Then I crept quietly through my brothers' bedroom and into the dining room.

'Is there going to be an air raid?' I asked when my father replaced the earpiece on its hook. If there was, I would have to dress quickly, sling my gas mask over my shoulder, ram my steel helmet onto my head, and cycle at top speed to the air raid control centre set up in St Martin's Hall, where I was listed as a mobile messenger. 'Mobile' meant bicycle-mounted.

'No. Nothing like that,' my father replied somewhat absent-mindedly, and then added softly:

'You can go back to bed.'

'But I'm awake now.'

'Then I suggest you get dressed. You can help me feed the chickens.'

He turned back to the telephone, lifted the cone-shaped black earpiece off its hook, and vigorously cranked the handle mounted on the right side of the wooden box.

'Mary?' He spoke into a black mouthpiece protruding from a hinged bracket on the front of the box. 'Mary? … Can you put me through to one four zero zero?'

I edged out of the dining room, closing the door slowly and deliberately, as if I did not want to disturb my sleeping brothers. But really I wanted to hear what my father was saying: I had recognized the number as the Guernsey Press where my father worked, and sensed something particularly newsworthy must have happened for him to call his office so early.

'Hullo? Jack? It's Stan.' His voice was muted now, heard through the door. 'I've been talking to Mr Peake. We'll have to reset the whole front page…. All of it…. Yes, the advertisements, too; they'll have to go…. We'll run the presses early, as soon as the front page is locked up…. And, Jack: Keep your eye on the Creed, in case anything else comes in.'

The Creed, I knew, was a recently acquired teletype-like machine which fed news out on a long thin strip of paper. Some very important news must have come in for my father to strip the whole front page. But what?

I trod quietly back to my bedroom, pulled on my

school uniform, and made up my bed. In the passage leading to the back door, I balanced on each foot in turn as I pushed the other foot into a wellington boot. Then I stepped down into the glassed-in conservatory tacked onto the rear of the bungalow, to measure and mix the chicken mash. As I worked I caught fragments of subdued conversation filtering through the partly open kitchen window.

'Shall I send them to school?' (That was my mother).

'I would.' My father's voice was even huskier than usual. 'Act as if it's just a normal day.'

'Ian, too?'

'I should think so.'

'He's only nine.'

'I'll take him with me, in the car. And pick him up.'

'What will you tell them?'

'I'll not. It would be wrong to hear it from me.'

'Shall I, then?'

'No. The news was given only to me, to publish today.'

'Then what difference does it make from whom they hear it?'

'Let them hear at school. Like all the other boys.'

'It would be better coming from us.'

'No. I can't risk it. No one else knows. Just Jack Loftus—he took the message off the Creed—and Frank Peake and the Bailliff....'

There was a pause. I thought they might have sensed I was within earshot and had moved into the front room.

What is it we're going to be told? I wondered. *And why do we have to wait? Why all the secrecy?*

I was about to carry the galvanized pail of mash out to the chicken coop when the voices started again. 'When will you be home?' I heard my mother ask. From the choked-up sound of her voice I suspected she had been weeping—a rare occurrence.

'As soon as the paper's put to bed.'

'Will you go back?'

'If I have to. It depends. I'll talk to Peake.'

'You'll not stay?'

'In Guernsey?'

I couldn't hear my mother's reply.

'It would be unwise,' my father said.

They must have moved away from the window, for the voices were hushed for a few moments. Then I caught a few more fragments.

'How soon will it happen?'

'Tomorrow, I expect. Children will go first. Then men of conscription age and the elderly—those who want to leave. And the women and....'

'We won't be able to go together?'

'I doubt it.'

'Not as a family?'

Again there was no answer. I could imagine my father giving one of his characteristic shrugs: the gesture he used when he either did not know the answer to a question or—more often—preferred to remain noncommittal.

The heavy pail banged against my thigh as I dragged it down the cinder path. The hens saw me coming and fluttered to one end of the cage, cackling and pushing each other aside in their eagerness to be first to dip their beaks into the dry porridge-like mash.

So we're going somewhere, I thought as I lifted the heavy pail and sloshed its contents into the hip-high trough. *And it'll be tomorrow! But where? And why?*

I felt vaguely left out, ignored, a little miffed.

Surely, now I'm fifteen, I'm old enough to be told? I mean, I'm old enough to be a messenger, wearing my shrapnel helmet out on my bike in the air raids!

Part 2

Life in Guernsey
1925-1939

South Coast Cliffs; photo: Carel Toms

2

Early Years

Although I lived in Guernsey until I was fifteen, like many youngsters I seemed unaware of the beauty around me. I would cycle daily through narrow, winding lanes bordered by grass-covered earth banks dotted with primroses, violets, pink campion, cellandine, buttercups and field daffodils, which would stir in the breeze I created and lean toward me and nod as I glided past. I would amble along rough, winding gravel paths three hundred feet above the south coast bays, my sandals swishing against nettles, dock leaves, and long grasses. Thorny blackberry tendrils would grip my wool socks and I would have to pause and with careful fingers pry them away.

My ears would be besieged by the incessant screeching of gulls as they noisily claimed territory on cliff ledges. I would stop to watch an almost motionless gull hovering in the breeze beside me no more than six feet from my shoulder, its beady eye fixed upon me until, deciding I was not about to discard anything edible, it would dip its beak and in one swoop soar down to sea level and skim along the wave tops. I would peer over clumps of green and yellow gorse that clung to the upper cliffs, mesmerized by the surging motion of the sea as it crashed against the granite outcrops, throwing fragmented white spume high into the wind or, on calmer days, break into shallow rollers that glided up the beach and splashed gently onto the fine white sand.

In the late summer I would pause to pluck bulbous, juicy blackberries from thorn-spiked branches bent low to the ground, then scramble down steep, ragged paths to the rock-strewn beaches and clamber over still-wet boulders until I reached the soft sand accessible only at low tide. I would kick off my sandals and pull off my socks, chucking them high onto a rock where they would be safe from the incoming tide, then run the length of the beach splashing through shallow pools, savouring the feel of sand ridges under the soles of my feet. At the water's edge I would pause to roll my grey flannel shorts higher up my thighs and, kicking into each wavelet as it approached, push my way out until I was standing knee-deep in the chilly waters of the English Channel. I would remain perfectly still for minutes at a time, fascinated by the restless thrust of the sea as it ebbed and flowed, unaware that its pull one day would become an insistent call for me to return to my island; a call that would re-assert itself time and time again throughout my life.

Often I would spend a whole afternoon alone, intuitively aware that I would be unable to savour the experience, to reflect upon it, if accompanied by boys of my own age. They would be intent on clambering noisily up the nearby cliffs in search of gulls' eggs or crashing through the shallows in chase of sideways-scuttling crabs. They would create a disturbance, interrupt my reverie. (Thirty years later I would intentionally choose to travel unaccompanied to the island, preferring to re-create the experiences of my childhood privately rather than try to explain my intimate relationship with the lanes, cliffs, bays, and particularly the sea. Now, sixty years later, I have learned to share these experiences, for when I am gone who will know they ever existed?)

My parents owned an asbestos-walled frame bungalow in La Bellieuse, beside an unnamed lane that wound around St Martin's church and up a slight incline. From the gravelled driveway that dropped steeply into the lane I could turn right, toward Les Merriennes and eventually the town of St Peter Port; or left, downhill, to the high moss-covered granite wall that bounded the graveyard surrounding the church. From there it was only a few turns of my pedals into the winding lanes of Les Hubits; lanes that, on sunny summer afternoons when I was about six, my mother would sometimes take me and my two younger brothers for an afternoon picnic.

'I've got a good hayfield ready for your boys, missus,' Mr Mauger would announce as he tipped a round, brass-coloured Guernsey milk can over a pint jug held out by my mother. Morning and evening, Mr Mauger delivered still-warm milk from his herd of Guernsey cows. 'The hay could do with some turning,' he would add, and he would incline his head and wink at the two boys peering at him from behind their mother's skirts.

That afternoon she would pile a tea basket and a blanket into the pram beside baby Ian, and wheel it down La Bellieuse into Les Hubits, an older boy on either side of her. The two boys, who then were six and four, would each grip the pram handle with one hand and let the other hand—the lanes were so narrow—drift through the long grasses sprouting from the hedges (but with a wary eye alert for embedded stinging nettles!).

Their mother would spread the blanket in a corner of the field and lay the baby on it. The two boys would strip off their outer clothes, down to the black bathing suits (with bib-like fronts and straps stretching over their shoulders) they had pulled on before leaving home, and hurl themselves into the deep, golden hay. They would throw it at each other, pile it into forts, burrow secret tunnels, and chase after field mice, until their mother called them back to the blanket.

They would sit cross-legged, a Hovis-bread sandwich filled with Marmite and watercress grasped between their fingers, and a mug of lemonade balanced in the hay beside them. As they munched they would eye the Huntley and Palmer biscuit tin which, although their mother always teasingly professed contained only plain Arrowroot biscuits, they correctly guessed really held little iced cakes or Lyons' miniature chocolate rolls wrapped in glittering silver paper.

When they were finished they would ask if they could 'please leave the table'—and point to the blanket and giggle at each other—then dive back into the hay, knowing their mother would soon call them to get dressed. There would be pleas to stay longer, and always she would say yes; but with a raised finger she would caution them: 'Just five minutes, mind!'

Again they would hurl themselves back into the hayfield, until their mother called a third time. This time they knew to return without demur.

The little band would wind its way slowly homeward, the boys sunburned and scratching, itchy from the hay stalks that had dug into their skins. Their mother would laugh: 'You look for all the world as though you've caught twenty-four-hour chicken pox!'

They would stop and look each other up and down, and they would giggle, sharing the moment. They would walk on eagerly, knowing that when their mother turned the pram around the corner at the foot of La Bellieuse, they could scamper ahead up the incline to Wendy Cotte and try to be the first to run up to their father and thrust their bare, spotty arms in front of him, pretending they had caught a mysterious disease. He would peer at the spots and pretend to be concerned, gravely asking them if they might be infectious, and perhaps even suggesting he should take them to see the doctor.

"No. Don't be silly," the younger brother would chirp, not quite sure whether his father was being serious. "We've been playing in the hayfield!"

*

We were a family of five: my parents Marjorie and Stanley, and their three sons Ronald, Anthony and Ian. With the exception of Marjorie, we were all Guernsey born.

Marjorie came to the island with her parents in 1921. Her father, Captain George Steele, was an education officer with the British Army who had served in (what was then) northern India, Egypt, Cyprus, Malta, and County Cork in Ireland, and his family had travelled with him.

His wife's name was Bertha and she had just turned 19 when they were married near Portsmouth in 1867. The very next day they travelled to Plymouth in an old steam train, where they embarked on a troopship that took three weeks to reach India. She shared a cabin with two other officers' wives on an upper deck at the rear of the ship, while her new husband, who then was a second lieutenant, shared a cabin with other officers near the bow, where they could keep an eye on the troops.

When they got to India she had to board another train, densely crowded and much smellier and dustier than the first, which chugged noisily toward the Punjab foothills. When it reached the end of the line she was invited to climb onto the back of a donkey and bumped along uncomfortably for several days until they reached a remote Army outpost at Peshawar. Her four children, three sons and finally a daughter, were all born there.

He was serving in County Cork when, in 1921, he reached retirement age. He and Bertha chose to retire to Guernsey where he could work as a teacher with the Boys Intermediate School, and took their daughter Marjorie with them to live in a square three-storey granite row house called 'Halcyon' in Doyle Road, just around the corner from the school where he would teach (by then their three sons had all chosen to emigrate to Canada).

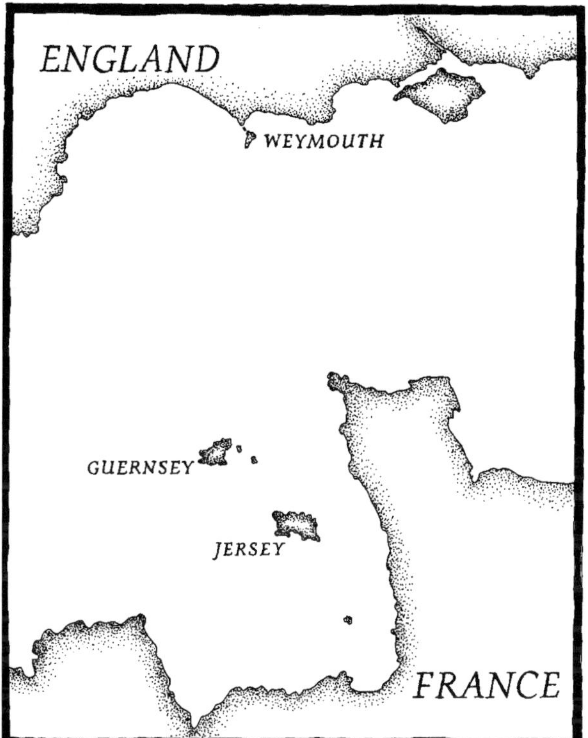

The Channel Islands are significantly closer to France than England

Marjorie had loved living in County Cork and fussed her parents interminably about their choice of Guernsey. But her father insisted: intuitively, he could foresee the troubles that would erupt between Britain and what eventually was to become Eire. So she heaved a petulant sigh, agreed he might be right, and sailed across the English Channel determined not to like the island. Yet, reluctantly, she had to admit the scenery and the lifestyle appealed to her. She felt Guernsey was like Malta, where she lived in her mid-to-late teens: both were surrounded by water, both were hilly, and in both many of the residents spoke another language. She had simply traded Malta's barren rocks, dust and burnt colours for Guernsey's gorse-covered cliffs, mist and lush greenness.

She met her future husband at a tennis gala in Richmond Park, and as their friendship matured he encouraged her to ride beside him in the sidecar attached to his motor bike. Later, he taught her to ride a motor bike of her own, until one sunny Sunday afternoon she approached a T-junction too fast and shot over both the handlebars and the turf hedge that arrested her progress. (In later years, when relations between my parents were sometimes strained, as a teen-age boy I would ponder how two people with such diverse backgrounds and interests could possibly have been attracted to one another.)

My father—Arthur Stanley Blicq—was a true Guernseyman, born and brought up on the island and the sole remaining member of his side of the family. In his youth he was known as Sandy because of his light coloured hair, but I never heard my mother call him anything but Stan. We were told his father had died in Africa in the Boer War, his mother had died in London during an influenza epidemic, and his sister had taken a boat to America in 1920 and was never heard from again. From the age of eight he had been brought up by Priscilla Ereaux, his grandmother on his mother's side, and she had no surviving family either. But with the birth of his first son—and later two more—he was indeed a happy man. Now he knew the family name would endure.

Their three sons were Ronald Stanley (born in 1925), Anthony Norman (1926), and Ian Herbert (1930). When Ronald and Anthony were born the family lived in a small cottage in Calais, near Icart cliffs, until a fire destroyed much of the building. (I have a very early memory of my father carrying his grandmother Priscilla, who lived with us then, loudly voicing her disapproval on being removed from her upstairs bedroom and being unceremoniously dumped on the front lawn while smoke billowed from the windows until the fire brigade arrived.) Shortly thereafter they moved into Wendy Cotte—named by my mother—in La Bellieuse, the bungalow I remember distinctly and which features in this memoir.

Stanley had trained as a journalist and had been a sports writer for the *Guernsey Evening Press*—natural for him because he was an ardent and well-known soccer player. When I was quite young he would take me to watch soccer matches, which we viewed from the Press booth while he wrote his report. Later, sports were covered by others because he became an editor and eventually chief editor.

It was into this setting that I was born and grew up until my mid-teens. It was an easy-going, relaxed environment with few restrictions, far different from the environment most children experience today. We were free to roam wherever we wanted and whenever we liked, with no cautions to avoid certain areas or not to speak to strangers. The only constraints seemed to be that we should dress appropriately, be prompt at mealtime, and after tea be home by a prescribed time, ready to wash our faces, brush our teeth, and climb into our beds.

3

A Day at the Beach

The family's black Rover four-door sedan dipped its nose at the top of the steep, winding hill that dropped 300 feet from Pleinmont Road down to Rocquaine Bay. Immediately the two boys kneeling on the back seat (who had been peering expectantly out of a window on each side waiting for just the right moment) began to chant in unison: 'I can see the sea! I can see the sea!' Over and over again.

Their father smiled and glanced into the rear-view mirror. His eldest son—now nine—was sitting behind him gripping the window ledge and staring toward the grey line on the horizon that marked the junction of sea and sky. Beside him, on the other side of the car, seven-year-old Tony was jumping up and down in time with his chanting. Between them, Joey—their brown sort-of Cocker Spaniel—sat with his head cocked to one side, his stubby tail thumping against the back of the seat. It was Sunday, the only day the boys' father did not have to go to the *Guernsey Press* newsroom, and he was driving his family to their favourite beach: Portelet Bay.

From the front seat, three-year-old Ian chimed in with his own chant, more or less in time with the others: 'I see sea! I see sea!' His mother jogged him

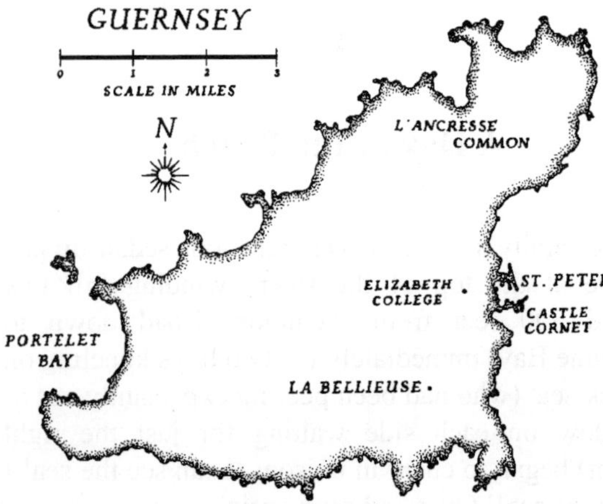

on her lap in time with the chant, and the boys' father smiled again.

But the eldest boy's chant evaporated when the Rover turned the last corner that would bring them onto the road that skirted the sea wall. Already the familiar iodine taint of seaweed drying on the beach mingled on his tongue with the acrid fear of the ordeal to come.

It was the slipway at Portelet Bay that created a problem. A private problem not understood by the rest of his family—if they were even aware of it.

Like most of Guernsey's beaches, access to Portelet was down a slipway—a ramp—built in the 1800's of brick-sized chunks of steel-grey granite laid in parallel rows across its width. Each row of bricks was tilted so that its uphill edge was raised just enough to form a ridge for hooves and wheels to grip as fishermen drove their two-wheel horse carts up the slope.

At Portelet the slipway was about 200 feet long, steeply inclined, and on the landward side butted against a nearly vertical cliff bank. The top of the slipway was 40 feet above a rocky beach, and for a short distance it had a low protective wall on its outer edge to prevent vehicles from rolling off. But for the remaining distance—about 160 feet—there was no protective wall. And that final stretch worried me.

The entrance to the slipway was approached by a right-angled turn off the Pleinmont Road, and then another immediate right-angled turn in the opposite direction. My father would reverse into the entrance, negotiate the two turns, and then back down the slipway. Often, cars were already parked against the cliff on the upper part of the slope, with boats and round wicker lobster pots stacked behind them, so he would have to find space near the bottom, which meant travelling along the outer edge of the slipway to get there. I was obsessed by the fear that the brakes would fail, or we would drive too near the edge and the wheels would slip over and the car would plunge to the sand below.

My fear was not confined to the slipway at Portelet. I experienced it just as acutely when we drove onto the quay at St. Peter Port to watch the mailboats come in, or parked beside the model yacht pond on the pier that extended out to sea toward Castle

Cornet. I would start to tremble silently in the back seat. In my mind I could see the front of the car butting into the single steel cable that stretched at knee height from bollard to bollard along the sea wall; I could hear the cable snapping and recoiling as it curled in each direction toward the bollards; and I could feel the bottom of the car scrape against the edge of the wall as it slid forward and toppled into the water far below. I had no fear of drowning, for I was a confident swimmer (the difficulty the family would experience in trying to extricate themselves from a sinking car had not yet become part of my problem); it was simply the fear of falling that troubled me, a fear that would haunt me for the rest of my life.

The sequence at Portelet was nearly always the same.

'Let me see if there is space on the slipway,' I would suggest, my hand already on the door handle as the car approached the refreshment kiosk at the top of the bay.

'Oh, there'll be plenty of room,' my father would say, drawing to a stop just beyond the entrance and shifting into reverse gear.

'Well, I can guide you down, then,' I would respond, almost too quickly, my knuckles white as I gripped the door handle.

Occasionally my father would agree, but more often he would say: 'I can manage, thank you,' probably feeling safer with me inside than outside the car. It was one less factor to contend with as he negotiated the descent.

I would sit in terror, torn between kneeling on the seat facing backward, so I could see through the rear window and warn my father if the wheels wandered too close to the unprotected edge, or sitting by the door, with my hand on the door handle, ready to leap out at the first sign of a calamity.

If I knelt on the seat I would likely be reprimanded: 'Get your head down! I can't see!' If I stayed in my seat, or was commanded to sit, I would grip the front edge of the seat with my free hand and, as the back of the car dipped slightly after twisting around the S-bend, I would plant both feet firmly on the floor and, with each bump over the rough cobbles, would press down harder and harder, as if by so doing I could will the car to slow down. Sometimes a cautionary 'Not too fast' or 'We're too close to the edge' would escape my lips, which would wring an irritated admonishment from my father: '*All right!*' Or—worse—there would be an exasperated 'That's enough of that!' from my mother.

The pressure exerted on the balls of my feet would set up a nervous shaking of my knees, which would accelerate uncontrollably throughout my body. Not until the car had come to a complete stop and my father had applied the handbrake was I able to release the pressure and stop the trembling. Immediately I would open the door and jump out, to prevent my brother, or—worse—my parents, from noticing my disgusting fear. Now I could push to the back of my mind the thought that at the end of the day the car still had to be driven up the slipway. Portelet offered so much, and evening was a long time away.

Portelet Bay was named after Portelet Harbour, its most significant feature, and was pronounced the Guernesiaise way: *Port-a-lay*. The bay faced north and curved in a shallow arc from the slipway at one end to a promontory of boulders and seaweed-strewn rocks at the other, beyond which a series of rocky inlets extended westward to Pleinmont Point. At the back of the bay a three-foot-high granite wall restrained the base of the steep cliff of reddish earth, coarse grass, and yellow gorse, and prevented it from encroaching upon the broad strip of soft, white, pebble-free sand. Shapeless strips of dried *vraic* (the patois name for seaweed), small pebbles, and broken shells formed a fragmented line that separated the dry sand on which picnickers sat and the damp sand upon which the sea encroached twice a day.

Although a few of the picnickers were visitors to the island, most were from the neighbouring country parishes of Torteval and St. Saviour. On Sunday afternoons they sat in family groups of 12 to 15: parents, grandparents, aunts, uncles, and children, many of the adults still dressed in their Sunday best, and the little girls—for there seemed to be far more girls than boys—in crisp white or flowered dresses and white ankle socks. All of them spoke the Island patois known as *Guernesiaise*.

Opposite: Portelet Bay, with the harbour at top right. The cluster of rocks and pools is half way up the beach, at the left of the photograph. The slipway is immediately below the photographer's position. Photo by Carel Toms.

The sand below the tide line was speckled with pebbles in granite hues of rusty red, brown, and grey. In the middle there was a cluster of low, smooth, hump-backed rocks which, when the sea receded, enclosed tiny pools containing a microcosm of sea life waiting to be released when the waves again swept inward. Farther down the beach craggy rocks thrust out of the water for an hour or two at low tide, thick bands of brown vraic hanging limply from their crevices, only to disappear from view soon after the tide turned and the water again began to rise.

Portelet harbour was on the west side of the beach, in an inlet between two great banks of rock. The harbour wall was L-shaped and stood eight feet high at its seaward end, its boulders piled one above the other with, on the top, a light covering of cement that served as an uneven path. As the tide came in and the water level rose within the harbour, children would stand atop the wall—my brothers and I among them—each unwinding lengths of coarse green line from the hand-held fishing reels peculiar to the island: four five-inch lengths of wood joined at their ends to form a rectangle, with the line wound from one side to the other. A metal ring tied to the end of the line served as a weight and pulled the two hooks down into the water.

The fisher folk would lean over, peering into the depths and adjusting their lines so that the limpet bait concealing the hook would dangle just an inch or so from the granite boulders beneath their feet. Small fish would dart out eagerly and nibble at the pieces of limpet and the children would quiver in anticipation.

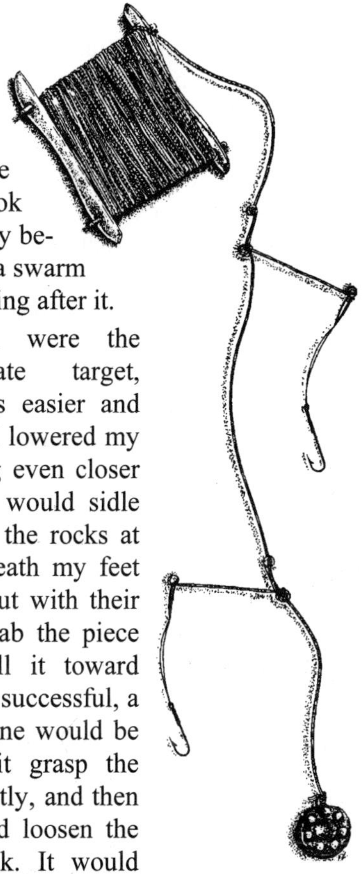

A Guernsey fishing line

But often, to their chagrin, a larger fish would drag the whole piece of limpet off the hook and fishtail hurriedly be-between the rocks, a swarm of smaller fish chasing after it.

Although fish were the children's ultimate target, catching crabs was easier and often more fun. If I lowered my line so that it hung even closer to the wall, crabs would sidle out to the edge of the rocks at varying levels beneath my feet and would reach out with their claws, trying to grab the piece of limpet and pull it toward them. If a crab was successful, a gentle tug on the line would be enough to make it grasp the piece of limpet tightly, and then a firmer pull would loosen the crab from the rock. It would wrap its other claws around the line, then I would give a gentle upward pull and haul the crab up and over the harbour wall, its claws waving in the air, surprised at its sudden predicament.

I would lower the crab onto the surface of the wall, place a thumb and a forefinger lengthwise across its back—which sometimes measured as much as five inches across—and grasp the crab at the outer edges of its shell. With the other hand I would hold the hook and gently prise it loose from the greedy claws. Then, with its claws waving frantically beneath my hand, I would hold the crab up for the younger, and sometimes older, onlookers to inspect before lowering it into a water-filled bucket.

At the end of each fishing expedition I would lower my catch alive into the sea—it was an island tradition. As I upended the bucket I would watch the small fish wriggle away and the crabs sink to the sandy bottom. There they would scramble over each other as they scuttled back toward the protection of the harbour wall.

As evening approached the sun would drop toward the far end of the bay and the cliff's shadow would creep across the beach. A breeze would spring up and the women would pull cardigans over their sleeveless dresses. But the children playing in the rock pools, building sand-and-rock dams in an attempt to prevent the approaching waves from encroaching on their territory, and those fishing from the harbour wall, would be oblivious to the change in temperature and would turn deaf ears to their parents' calls for them to 'Come and get changed now; it's time to go home.'

I admit now, that when it was time to go home I was the worst dawdler on the beach. I would call back that I had to turn over just one more rock (in my never-ending search for tiny crabs to place in the pool I had dammed between two rock outcrops), or that I needed to pile one more bucketful of sand onto the dam I was building (to increase its resistance to the waves that shortly would lap against it), or that I had to rewind the wet string of my fishing line (because it had got all tangled up).

I paused to glance up the beach. Young Ian was standing beside his mother, his white buttocks bare as she rubbed him down with a towel. Tony had draped a towel round his waist while he kicked off his black bathing suit, and was tugging at the belt of his short trousers as he tried to haul them up over his still damp, sand-covered legs. My father had folded the deck chairs into a pile and was shaking sand out of the blanket and wet towels. And Joey was digging furiously with his front paws, his damp tummy dragging on the pile of sand he had excavated while his back legs kicked sand onto the picnic basket.

'Stop that dog, will you Stan!' I heard my mother say.

And then my father's voice: *'Joey!'*

The dog paused briefly to look up, and then continued digging.

My father picked up a stone and hurled it toward the water. 'Here, Joey! Fetch it!' The dog chased after it.

Around them other groups were packing up and straggling across the beach toward the slipway, carrying deck chairs, picnic baskets, blankets, and clothing rolled into bundles.

I sat on a rock, brushing sand from my arms and legs in a desultory fashion. I gazed at two fishermen as they anchored their boat and splashed in the shallows in their long sea boots, hauling flat boxes and wicker crates onto a wooden cart they had rolled into the water. So far they had brought in seven boxes.

My mother's voice broke into my thoughts: 'Oh, do get *on!*' she called. 'Tony's almost dressed!'

Trust Tony to be setting an example! I ran up the beach, kicking sand ahead of me. I stood beside him and pulled the straps of my black bathing suit over my shoulders, slipping my arms out of the loops, and rolled the top down, taking care that it still covered my navel. From the pile of clothing lying on the sand I pulled out an aertex sleeveless vest, slipped it over my head, and thrust my fists through its armholes.

'I've told you before,' my mother admonished, sounding each word one at a time, like a teacher repeating instructions to a class of inattentive children: 'Take your bathing suit right off *before* you put on your vest, otherwise you'll get the bottom wet.'

I reached for the towel lying in a loop around my feet and pulled it up, wrapping one side round my middle, above the bathing suit, and letting the vest fall outside it.

I paused to watch the fishermen, who had hauled their cart out of the shallows and were attaching a long cable to the back of an old Austin that stood farther up the beach. They climbed in and started to drive slantwise across the damp sand, heading for the slipway, the cart bouncing and clattering as its ironclad wooden wheels trundled over the scattered pebbles.

'See if they've got any mackerel, will you Stan,' my mother called.

My father stopped shaking out the towel he was holding and walked toward the approaching fishermen, folding the towel as he went.

This would be fun! I hastily shoved my feet into my shorts and underpants and pulled them up, for once not worrying that my bottom was still damp and the underpants were sandy and scrunched up. I cast off the towel and ran down the beach, stepping nimbly onto the little sand patches between the pebbles, trying to do up my fly buttons as I ran. My two brothers chased after me.

The old Austin lurched to a stop. My father leaned into the car window and then stepped back as one of the fishermen opened the door and walked back to the cart.

'Plenty of mackerel,' I heard the fisherman say. 'A few whiting. And both crabs and lobsters.'

Tony and I placed our hands on the top edge of the cart and peered over at the silvery-grey mackerel and greeny-blue lobsters, the latter casting claws and feelers searchingly out of a large basket.

'Ooh!' we gasped, and withdrew our fingers.

'Let me see! Let me see!' Ian shouted, reaching up with his hands and grasping the wooden slats along the side of the cart.

I tucked my hands under Ian's armpits and lifted him until his nose was high enough to see over the edge. 'Don't put your fingers near!' I cautioned, and he lowered his hands and crossed the palms behind his back.

Our father turned to me: ‘Ronald, run up and ask Mummy if she wants a lobster.’

Lowering Ian to the sand, I ran about twelve steps up the beach and stopped. ‘Mummy!’ I shouted. ‘Daddy says do you want a lobster?’

My mother nodded and held up two fingers. ‘She says to buy two,’ I called to my father, and ran the few short steps back to the cart.

‘I said to run up and *ask* her,’ my father corrected me. ‘Not to shout it so the whole beach can hear. *I* could have done that.’ And then he added. ‘You haven’t got your sandals on yet. Run down to the water’s edge and soak this towel. Wring it out so it’s still wet but doesn’t drip.’

By now the incoming tide had brought the water nearer. I walked into it almost knee deep and swirled the towel around without embedding sand in it, and then ran back with the ends of the towel flapping wetly against my shins.

My father took one end while I held the other, between us forming a hammock. The fisherman lifted a lobster from the basket, holding it between thumb and fingers stretched across the curved green back, and held it up with the claws and feelers searching aimlessly in the air. My two brothers stepped back. (I would have done the same had I not been holding the towel.) Our father nodded and the fisherman lowered the lobster into the hammock; I leaned as far back as my arms would permit. The fisherman selected a second lobster and placed it beside the first. My father drew the two ends of the towel together to form a damp sling.

'Who wants to carry this?' he asked.

The three boys eyed the tapered feelers poking out around the edge of the towel and backed away.

Our father laughed.

'How much do I owe you?' he asked the fisherman.

'Two bob each for the lobsters, and ninepence each for the mackerel. That'll be six and three.'

My mother eyed the catch and then sent me back to the water's edge to soak a second towel to wrap the mackerel in. And then she sent me back a third time, to rinse out my bathing suit.

'You're not taking it home like that,' she said. 'The sand will get all over the house. And while you're about it, you can wash the sand off your feet. Take your towel with you.'

I started toward the water.

'Take your sandals, too!' she called after me. 'You'll only get your feet sandy again, when you come back up the beach.'

Half way down the beach, I stopped beside the cluster of rocks with their embedded pools and placed my sandals and towel on a flat rock. Then I walked farther down the beach and waded knee-deep into the sea, vigorously swirling the bathing suit around my knees.

I wrung it out, splashed back through the shallows toward the cluster of rocks, laid it beside my sandals, and perched my buttocks on another rock with a pool beside it, dangling my feet in the sun-warmed water. A purple sea anemone shrunk into itself and a small, pale crab, hardly an inch across, scuttled away and buried itself in the sand at the bottom of the pool.

Reaching into the pool, I fished out a smooth stone and cradled it in the palm of my hand, wrapping my thumb along one edge and curling my forefinger around another. Clinging to the rocks around me were several pyramid-shaped limpets, varying from half an inch to one-and-a-half inches across, all waiting for the tide to wash around them so they could move about, much as a snail moves along a wall.

A Guernsey limpet

The trick with limpets, I knew, was to take them by surprise. Normally, the mollusc housed within the shell gripped the rock surface with only moderate tension. But even the slightest touch on the extremely hard, ribbed, ochre-yellow shell would forewarn it of impending danger and in a fraction of a second the mollusc would cling so fiercely that the limpet could not be pried off the rock, even with a knife. A short, sharp, sideways swipe with a stone, before the limpet suspected it was about to be attacked, was the only way to shake its grip. But if the limpet was hit ineffectively it was useless to try any further; additional swipes would only crack or splinter the shell.

I surveyed the eight or nine limpets within reach and selected a large one to my right. Bracing my feet firmly on the opposite rock I leaned back slightly and swung my arm swiftly forward in an arc. But the stone hit the limpet only a glancing blow and immediately the mollusc tightened its grip. I selected a second limpet, moved myself to the left to gain a better swing, leaned back, and swung the stone toward it. This time the limpet skittered down the side of the rock and with a small splash came to rest wedged in a crevice about two inches below the surface of the pool.

I leaned forward and eased the limpet gently from the fissure. I turned it over, letting it rest mollusc-side-up in the palm of my hand and placed a fingertip lightly on its dark centre to feel its firmness. The dark area in the middle extended almost to the shell and was encircled by a narrow band of pale, milky, but still firm flesh. At one end—for limpets are oval—there were two darker patches side by side and close together. Almost like eyes, I thought, though I knew they were not.

Looking at the limpet in my hand, I knew why I found killing them so distasteful. It couldn't be done cleanly. You couldn't hit it over the head and know it was dead; indeed, there was no way you could tell a live limpet from a dead limpet. So how did you know if you were causing it pain? I had seen the country boys use knives to cut inside the oval edge of the shell and scoop out the whole mollusc, lay it on a rock, and dice it into bait-size pieces. But at what moment did it die? When did those 'eyes' stop watching you? I didn't own a knife—my parents would not allow it—and so had to borrow pieces of bait from boys who performed the act for me. And on one occasion, when no one else was around, I had swiped a limpet from the side of a rock, laid it face down on the wall, and with repeated blows had smashed the shell and crushed the mollusc into shredded pieces that were difficult to pull apart and had little bits of shell adhering firmly to them. (It reminded me of trying to break the pieces of shell off a hard-boiled egg.) Then I had to impale the lump of mixed flesh and shell onto a hook, which looked neither professional nor effective. It was a disgustingly messy business, and as soon as the sun began to dry the soft part of the limpet its flesh began to smell atrociously. I never tried it again.

A sharp, imperious voice interrupted my reverie. 'What are you *doing?* Everyone else is ready to go!'

My mother was standing with one arm wrapped around a rolled blanket and her other hand holding her sandals by the heels. Where the blanket had lain now consisted only of a patch of flattened sand with, beside it, my jersey and fishing line. My father had returned from placing the fish and lobsters in the car and was already trudging back through the loose sand toward the slipway with the picnic basket in one hand and a tomato chip in the other. The chip was a wooden basket containing the remnants of the tea he had bought from the kiosk at the top of the slipway: an empty teapot, hot water jug, milk jug, sugar basin, and two tea cups. Little Ian trotted beside him, one hand grasping the handle of the tomato chip.

Half way between them and my mother, Joey was pulling Tony toward the slipway. Tony had paused at the sound of his mother's voice, the dog quivering as the lead tightened. He looked first at his mother and then at his tardy brother. 'We'll go without you,' he shouted, anticipating his mother's next words.

'I'm going up to the car now,' she called. 'You'd better hurry up or we'll leave without you.'

I lowered the limpet into the pool, resting the mollusc face down against a rock so it could mould itself onto the surface. I dipped one foot into the water, rubbed a towel over and around it, and pulled a reluctant sandal over my still-damp heel. I glanced up the beach: my mother was nearing the foot of the slipway and had turned to watch me. I dipped my other

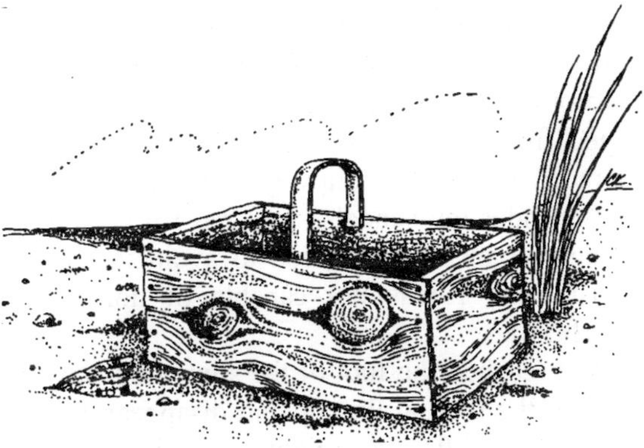

A Guernsey tomato chip.

foot into the water and repeated the drying and shodding. Grabbing the towel, I ran up the beach, my unbuckled sandals flip-flopping on the stones until I reached the dry sand, where granules collected under the soles of my bare feet and each step tended to pull the sandals off. I sat on the sand beside my jersey, shook out each sandal in turn, pulled it back on, and then did up the buckle.

I looked toward the slipway: my mother was standing beside the car and everyone else was in it. 'We're going now!' she called.

'I'm coming!' I shouted back, and saw my mother open her door.

I stood up, shook the sand out of my towel, and looked around for my bathing suit. I had left it on the rock!

Bundling the damp towel under my arm, I grabbed the fishing line and ran down the beach. From the slipway I could hear the whir of the car's starter, followed first by the sudden racing of the engine and then a quieter purr as my father pushed in the choke. I jumped from rock to rock, grasped the bathing suit, and raced toward the slipway, mindless now of the pebbles under my sandals. As I ran I tried rolling the bathing suit inside the towel, to avoid the inevitable criticism that I was not capable of doing the job properly.

As I reached the foot of the slipway, I saw the car turn onto the road at the top and disappear around the bend. I was a little overweight and had pudgy legs, so by the time I was half way up the slipway I was puffing. At the top I was gasping, partly from being out of breath and partly from fear—fear that my father, urged on by my mother 'to teach me a lesson'—might just for once have driven away without me. (He would wait farther along the road, I knew, but the fear remained just the same.)

As I rounded the corner I huffed a sigh of relief: the car was still there, standing beside the kiosk. I *knew they wouldn't*, I thought, padding heavily up to the left rear door and pulling it open.

'Mind the lobsters!' Tony warned from the far side of the back seat, his feet tucked tightly under him, beyond the reach of the lobster feelers protruding above the wet towels on the floor.

I lifted my legs gingerly over the towels and threw myself onto the rear seat, tucking my sandals well back. There still might be recrimination, but at least I did not have to face the ordeal of driving up the slipway.

*

Throughout my adult life I have carried memories of Portelet Bay with me. I can see the fishermen's boats afloat in the harbour, in the perfect setting when only the upper three inches of the harbour wall are visible (see page 26). What little wind there is will be coming from behind the cliffs, leaving the beach and rocks in almost total calm. The sea reflects the stillness, its surface unruffled until, about one hundred and fifty yards out from the shore, a soft breeze reaches down and gently touches the water, creating light flecks that extend to the horizon. Tiny wavelets drift silently inward and plop lightly onto the sand, each encroaching minutely farther up the beach than the one before it.

But it is from the rocks and miniature valleys at the west end of the bay that I most feel the restless pull of the sea. There, despite the calmness of the water, the sea surges into the crevices with a gentle smacking and gurgling, and the brown seaweed that clings to the lower rocks streams first in one direction as the water flows in, then in the reverse direction as it ebbs, like long hair trailing behind a mermaid. And when there is no movement the seaweed hangs in unkempt tufts until the next surge releases it into another paroxysm of movement.

Later—many years later—I recognised that it is the sea's calm but restless, relentless, endless movement that has characterized the restlessness I have experienced as an adult. A pull far more subtle than that of a wind-whipped ocean bearing down on rocks in tempestuous fury.

4

Printer's Ink

Arrival of an item of world news was preceded by a gentle hum and then a hiss from a pipe strapped to the wall. Moments later a flap clamped onto the end of the pipe opened, accompanied by a louder hiss, plop, and bump, and a 2½ inch long brass capsule padded at one end popped out and clattered into a cage. Curled inside the capsule was a telegram that had travelled under the road from the Post Office on the other side of Smith Street, eighty yards up the hill. I reached into the cage, grasped the capsule, lifted it out, and placed it on the shelf. Pushing two fingers into it, I twirled them to tighten the curled paper and pulled out the telegram. Jumping down from my stool, I trotted across the office and stood at my father's elbow.

'From Reuters,' I announced importantly, proud that I could name the source, and with the palm of my hand flattened the telegram on his desk.

My father lifted his head and nodded. 'Just leave it there,' he muttered. 'Thanks.' And he turned back to the galley he was proofreading. He wasn't ignoring me, we both understood that. It was a routine we'd grown comfortable with.

There was a return pipe too, for empty capsules. When I opened its flap I could hear the hum of the compressors from across the road, and if I stuck my fingers into the opening I could feel the suction grasping at my knuckles. I pulled my hand back quickly and fed the empty capsule padded-end first into the pipe and dropped the flap.

My father was news editor of the *Guernsey Evening Press*. To my 11-year-old eyes, he was the epitome of the editors I had seen in films at the Regal Cinema: he had removed his suit jacket and hung it over the back of his chair, loosened his cuff links, and folded his shirt cuffs back half way up his forearms; serge plus-fours, buckled beneath the knee, gripped the tops of long brown socks; pens and pencils sprouted from an upper pocket of his brown waistcoat; a green eyeshade jutted out from his forehead, just beneath his hairline; and, as he marked up copy with a thick black pencil, he leaned his forehead on the palm of his left hand, his elbow resting on the desk.

He shared his office with three other newspaper people, all older than my father. Jimmy Irish was white haired and had an equally white bushy moustache that curled up at the ends with a flourish. My father said he was senior editor, but to me his only job seemed to be composing the crossword puzzle that appeared in the *Weekly Press and Advertiser*. I never saw him work at anything else. Billy Vaudin was chief reporter, round, beaming, and always dressed in a navy-blue suit with a gold watch chain stretched tightly across his stomach from one waistcoat pocket to the other. And Nellie Emmett was local events and family news reporter. In her past she had had a mild stroke which impaired her speech and caused the left side of her mouth to hang loosely. (My brother Tony and I thought she was demented and we used to whisper cruelly to each other about her deformity, and giggle at each other's derisory remarks. How I wish I could retract my youthful insensitivity).

When I tired of waiting for messages to burst out of the pipe, I climbed down from the stool I had dragged over to the cage and wandered along a narrow passage and down a steep, wooden, creaky staircase that led into the composing room at the back of the building. The acrid smell of hot metal and the incessant clicking and clacking of typesetting machines assailed my senses the moment I pushed open the door.

As the operators typed, thin slices of metal, each with a reverse-image letter on its end, dropped four feet down inside a vertical glass-covered sleeve and into a forward-sloping tray. Here they were jostled to form an evenly spaced line and then covered with molten lead to form a slug about two inches long and three-quarters of an inch deep, each slug representing one line of type. The cooling slugs slid one after the other into the sloping tray, gradually forming paragraphs and eventually complete columns of print.

I sidled along the narrow walkway between the composing machines and the windows, and stopped behind the third operator, chosen because I could see he had almost finished the article he was typesetting. Something about the mailboat *Isle of Sark* being towed into Southampton because it had damaged a propeller as it left The Solent.

His piece finished, the operator lifted the tray of print and carried it over to a flat table, where he pushed an inked roller over the raised letters. Then he placed a sheet of newsprint on the top, gently rubbing a clean, soft rubber roller over the paper. He did this twice, taking off two galley proofs, one of which he placed with the tray of type and the other he pinned to the original article and carried upstairs for proofreading.

I waited patiently until the operator returned to his seat, lit a Woodbine, expelled a stream of smoke toward the open window, and reached for an ink-stained mug half full of milky tea.

'What's your name, lad?' he asked, swinging his stool round to his right.

I told him, and he typed rapidly.

'Where do you live?'

'Wendy Cotte, in La Bellieuse,' and I added the parish and telephone number.

Again he typed, the machine chattering and jostling the letters. Three slugs slid one after another into the tray: *click-click-click.*

The operator lifted them out, ran the roller over them, and handed me a galley proof with my name and address embossed onto the paper, and then the three still-warm slugs (which I prized far more than the printed sheet), on which I could read:

Stanley Ronald George Blicq
Wendy Cotte, La Bellieuse
St Martin, Guernsey, Ph 5223

The inner half of the composing room was filled with waist-high slabs, called stones, on which lay heavy newspaper-page-size metal trays. These were the frames in which the assembled lines of type were placed, aligned, and interspersed with blank metal pieces to prevent the type from moving during printing. When all the type, advertisements, and photographic blocks had been correctly positioned, keys on the sides of the frame were tightened to lock all the parts in place. Now the heavy frame was carried to the press room and laid beside another on the Wharfdale press. This was the operation that most fascinated me.

Jack Loftus was in charge of the press and was assisted by a youth known in the trade as a printer's imp. Between them they locked the frames firmly on the Wharfdale's print bed and then stood one at each end of the machine. Jack hauled down on a long-handled switch and the two trays moved forward together, sliding under an ink roller that spread a fine film of ink over the raised print. As the double tray rolled back toward him, Jack slid the top sheet of a pile of double-page-size newsprint onto it. A second roller descended and gently pressed the paper onto the metal. Grippers grasped the sheet and lifted it onto a webbed metal frame that wafted the paper over the top of the press in a long, graceful arc, the edges of the paper fluttering in the self-made breeze. As the sheet descended on the other side of the press, the printer's imp grasped it and pulled it toward him, placing it on top of the growing pile of newsprint on the bench between him and the press.

The roll-chug-whirr-flutter sequence was repeated over and over until Jack's pile of newsprint was exhausted. Then he stopped the press and the two men removed the double frame and replaced it with another containing the backs of the two pages they had already printed. The new frames were locked into position, the pile of printed sheets was carried back to Jack's side of the machine, and the two men resumed their positions and printed the reverse side of the sheet, which would become part of that evening's newspaper.

This process lasted until 1938, when my father exuberantly confided to me that two innovations shortly would revolutionize how the Evening Press was published. First to arrive would be a Cossor press, which not only had automatic feed but also would fold the papers and 'jog' every twelfth paper as it came out of the press so that they could be counted off in dozens. The second would be the installation of a 'Creed' machine in his office which, like a teletypewriter, would churn out world news almost endlessly, in spurts, night and day. The Post Office would no longer have to propel capsules through a tube buried under the street.

At the time I empathized with his excitement, yet in later years I realized that the new technology had removed some of the fascination that printing has always held for me.

*

Traditionally, the 25th of December is a special day for children in Great Britain, and Guernsey was no exception. Yet it's Christmas Eve that I remember more clearly, because our parents established a simple, warm, family tradition which we repeated year after year.

At about 2:30 p.m. our mother would call to us to come in from the garden. 'Wash your hands and faces,' she would say, 'and get ready to go to town.'

She would check we looked smart and clean—Tony and I would wear our school blazers and Ian a grey-green jersey—and then she would shepherd us down the gravel path into La Bellieuse. We would turn right and walk around the corner to the bus stop at the top of Les Merriennes, agog with expectation for we knew what was about to happen.

Twenty minutes later the bus would deposit us outside the Town Church opposite the Victoria pier, from where we would walk a short distance up cobblestone High Street and turn left into the Commercial Arcade—a pedestrian mall lined with clothing, jewellery and shoe shops. Our target was Le Cheminant's, the largest shop in the Arcade and *a toy shop!* (How we boys envied young David Le Cheminant, who went to school with Tony: we imagined he had unlimited access to the most exotic and expensive toys imaginable.)

The shop was situated on a corner and had three wide windows on one side and two on the other. Ian, still holding onto his mother's hand, would drag her to the middle window on the long side so he could gaze at the model cars and aeroplanes. Tony would detach himself from the group and walk around the corner to gaze wistfully at the boxed sets of oil paints and oil pastels.

But I was given little time to window-gaze.

'Walk up to the Press,' my mother would say. 'Tell your father we're waiting.'

I would nod (the procedure was the same every year) and walk sedately—self-importantly—through the shoppers until I rounded the corner into the High Street and was out of my mother's view. Then I would break into a trot, stepping nimbly around islanders chatting in small groups or working their way down to the bus stops, until I reached the Boots-Le Riche's corner, and turn left to push up the steeper slope of Smith Street. I'd try to take the wooden steps up to the editorial office two at a time, pausing at the top just long enough so I would look to my father as if I wasn't hurrying, wasn't overly excited, when I pushed open the door.

'Ah!' he would say. 'I know why *you're* here!'

He would pull on his suit coat, dig in the pocket for his pipe, and turn to wish a Happy Christmas to any other editorial staff who were present (all done agonisingly slowly, I felt), and then we would start the walk back to the Arcade. Everyone in the street seemed to be in a jovial mood and many my father knew would pause to exchange seasonal greetings with him. Meanwhile I would hang around the periphery, mentally urging them to hurry! *This is Christmas Eve!*

Eventually we would turn into the Arcade and immediately I could see Tony standing at the same shop window, still eyeing the painting sets. Ian would release his mother's hand and run up to his father and drag him to the window to point to the Meccano set he hoped to find in the pillow case that would be standing at the foot of his bed tomorrow morning. My father would bend down beside him to see exactly what he was pointing at, and then look up briefly, over Ian's head, to exchange a glance with my mother. I would watch carefully, because the slightest nod or shake of her head would tell me whether she had bought what he wanted.

'Well, we'll have to see what Father Christmas has in mind,' my father would say, turning back to Ian. 'Did you tidy the toy cupboard in your room, like your mother said? He'll be sure to look in there.'

He'd release Ian's hand and walk around the corner to Tony, who would point to the box of oil paints he had been admiring.

'Hmmm! We'll have to see,' I'd hear my father say. 'Watercolours are easier to work with, don't you think? They don't dry out so easily and they're *lots* easier to clean up.'

My mother would drag Ian toward us and say: 'We should get into Le Noury's, Stan, before it fills up.'

Le Noury's was the family's favourite restaurant, famous among adults for its 'steak-and-kidney pie with chips' lunch, but more famous among us boys for its teas. We would tramp up the stairs, with Tony and me in the lead, to see if there was a table by the window so we could press our noses against it and, by craning our necks, still see into Le Cheminant's windows 30 yards down the Arcade.

There would be scones and jam, paste and cress sandwiches, Guernsey gâche spread with Guernsey butter, and—the moment we had been waiting for—a waitress bearing a two-tiered cake tray with slices of rich, dark Christmas cake and shortbread on the lower level, and little cakes cut into diamond, square and round shapes, covered entirely in pink, white, or chocolate icing, each sitting daintily inside a fluted white doily on the upper tier.

'Just one each,' my mother would caution us, but of course she would give in because it was Christmas Eve and my father would call the waitress over to replenish the upper level.

Sated, we would stumble down the stairs and out into the Arcade, where shopkeepers would be locking their doors and extinguishing the shop lamps. Yet the islanders still chose to stroll about, wanting to savour the moment.

It would be fully dark by now and my father would suggest to my mother that we should walk out onto the harbour wall to look at the lights of Castle Cornet shining on the water: a strategy designed partly to help us walk off the effects of our large tea and partly to help calm us boys down on such an exciting evening. We would head toward Victoria Pier, Tony walking in front with me, both chatting amiably, with my parents strolling more slowly behind. My mother would slide her hand under my father's arm and little Ian would grab his other hand. It was Christmas Eve and all was well with our world.

*

The first Christmas or two after we had moved to Canada my father tried to replicate the experience, but it was never the same. At -22C it was much too cold to stroll comfortably around the streets; in such a large city we really didn't know anyone with whom to stop and exchange greetings; and there was no Le Noury's, no thinly sliced bread and butter or dainty sandwiches, no gâche, no Guernsey butter, and no little iced cakes as we knew them. The nearest we could achieve was to visit the shelves of the toy department in the Hudson's Bay Company, and then have tea in the Georgian Room on the sixth floor. It was nice, but it wasn't the same, and after two years the family no longer tried to repeat the experience. They just stored it in their memories.

5

A Sea-Faring Lad He Would Be

On Saturday mornings, from the time I was 9 until I was 13—when I discovered that I had to attend school on Saturday mornings!—I regularly asked my father to waken me early. We would breakfast together while the rest of the family slept, and then climb onto the brown-leather seats of the black Rover tourer standing on the gravel drive beside the house. (It was the second Rover I could remember my father owning, the first being a square, boxy car built in 1932 with black, soft-leather panels on the *exterior* of all four doors.)

We drove in companionable silence most of the way, first down the steep slope of les Merriennes, then along the gentler slopes of Ville-au-Roi and The Grange, encountering little motor traffic other than lorries bound for the docks, all loaded with boxes of tomatoes and flowers.

My father broke the silence as he turned the Rover into Mount Row. 'Did you remember your library book?'

'Two,' I replied laconically, patting the satchel lying across my knees. 'I finished them both.' I would go to Guille-Alles Library later in the morning, before meeting my father for the drive home.

'John or Percy?' He knew I was addicted to sea stories and especially those written by John and Percy F Westerman. We had discussed more than once whether the two writers might be brothers, even though they wrote separately. I thought they must be, because there were similarities in the way they wrote.

'Percy,' I said, reaching into my school satchel and pulling out a navy blue book with a square drawing of a tramp steamer on the front cover, etched in pale yellow ink. I held it up: 'Leslie Dexter, Cadet.'

'Good story?'

'Yes.' I dropped the book onto my lap, and it flipped open to page 16. Leslie Dexter was about to be interviewed as a candidate for sea duties with the shipping line of Whatmough, Duvant and Company (many of Percy Westerman's sea stories were built around the same company and its fleet of 'Golden' merchant vessels: the *Golden Dawn, Golden Gain, Golden Vanity* and *Golden Effort*).

"Leslie Dexter was a youth of fifteen," I read. "He was rather dark-featured, with closely cropped brown hair. His eyes were deep grey, and set beneath heavy eyebrows. Undoubtedly he gave an observer the impression that he possessed bodily health and strength, and that at the same time he was of a serious and studious nature. Well-built and athletic he certainly was, but there was very little of a studious character about Leslie Dexter. He might be looking as grave as an owl when all the time he was planning some ingenious though generally innocuous form of mischief.

"Just now he *was* serious.

"Leslie wanted to go to sea. To quote his own words, he was 'frightfully keen on it'." *

And so was I, but with a difference. Where Leslie Dexter wanted to be a sea cadet, and at the end of his training would rise slowly through the ranks of the merchant marine as a ship's officer, and perhaps eventually become Master of his own ship, my heart was set on becoming a wireless operator—a 'Sparks.' But that was a secret I shared with no one. I had learned the danger inherent in sharing personal ambitions with my school friends, even with my own family: too often they were debunked or the pleasure was smothered by others' snide remarks.

We parked beside the World War Cenotaph at the top of Smith Street and then strode in silent companionship down the steep slope toward the Guernsey Press. My father was already pulling his pipe out of his waistcoat pocket.

'Be back by one,' he'd say. 'All right?'

I would nod and he would turn into the narrow doorway, beyond which was a steep flight of dark, uncarpeted wooden stairs leading up to the editorial office. As soon as the door closed I broke into a run, turning left at the foot of Smith Street and darting down the narrow, cobble-stoned Pollet until I emerged onto The Esplanade. To my left, the clock on top of the Weighbridge announced it was 8:56: the first mailboat would not have docked yet.

- Percy F Westerman, *Leslie Dexter, Cadet* (London: Blackie & Son Limited, c 1935), p 16.

I waited for a lorry to pass, my toes balanced on the edge of the high curb, then scampered across the road to the path beside the granite sea wall. Here I turned north, toward the Weighbridge, my satchel slung across my back and resting on my shoulder blades, a stocky figure dressed all in grey: grey shorts, grey knee-high wool socks that already had started to bunch around my ankles, a grey V-neck pullover trimmed with green, black and white—the colours of the Boys Intermediate school—and a grey cap. I climbed up onto the sea wall (an action that would be heavily censured by my parents, if they knew) and watched the activity in the inner basin. When the tide was in, there might be an expensive yacht visiting from France, although more often there were only local fishing boats with the occasional fisherman sitting in the well mending his nets or fiddling with the motor. When the tide was out, gulls and terns would strut among the canted fishing boats resting on the ribbed sand, their heads cocked to one side as they listened for life beneath their webbed feet.

I kept glancing back over my right shoulder, to see if a black ball had been hoisted on the mast atop Castle Cornet on the far side of the harbour. The ball would signal that the Great Western Railway mailboat had been sighted. In 1937 there were two sets of passenger ships that sailed between the south coast of England and Guernsey and Jersey. The Great Western Railway operated three 2100-ton steamers with single red and black funnels out of Weymouth, and the Southern Railway operated three similar-sized steamers, but with twin yellow and black funnels, out of Southampton.

The mailboats also carried express freight, mostly perishables and travellers' effects, including a few cars. This freight had to be lifted into and out of the holds by dockside cranes, and it had to be moved quickly to ensure the ship would depart on time. Tomato chips and cardboard boxes of flowers were already waiting to be loaded on the quay, stacked high on square wooden flats. (Tomato chips were wooden boxes about 14 inches long by 8 inches wide and 6 inches high, with a single curved handle arched over the top – see page 39.)

The crane would swing down with a four-strand octopus sling dangling from a lifting hook larger than my torso. Each strand terminated in a smaller hook which the dockers would slip deftly into one of the four rings on the flat. A chief docker would stand beside the hold and signal to the crane operator far above him to haul the flat up, swing it in a curving arc from the quay to the ship, and lower it swiftly into the depths of the dark hold. With further hand movements he would caution the crane operator to slow the vertical drop, and then direct him to position the flat left, right, ahead, or back, until it was grasped by dockers standing in the hold and steered into position. It would be lowered the last few critical inches, the octopus sling would droop, and the unseen dockers would slip the hooks out of the rings and into those of a flat waiting to be hoisted ashore. It was this loading and unloading that I chiefly came to see.

From the Weighbridge I ran along the harbour wall until I reached the New Jetty, puffing up the long flight of steps to the observation platform on the roof. The

Isle of Sark was signalling her arrival from Jersey with a long blast and a gush of steam from the whistle clamped to the front funnel. Already she was being eased toward the quay, about ten feet of churning water remaining between her steel-plated sides and the green, seaweed-covered uprights of the pier. Crew members on board the *Isle of Sark* threw heavy rope hawsers to the dockers on the quay, who looped them around bollards. On board, the ropes were wound around winches on the fore and aft decks, which clattered and groaned as they wound the rope in, lifting it from a long loop that drooped into the water to a tightly-stretched dripping hawser hung with errant pieces of seaweed.

From my vantage point on the visitors' platform I was level with the upper deck of the ship, a deck frequented by the ship's crew but out of bounds to passengers. Directly opposite me was a square, white, box-like structure, which I knew must be the wireless room: the Sparks's domain (I could tell by the wire leading up from a point beside the door to a cable strung between the masts). Inside I knew there would be a bench along one wall, on it a receiver with a large tuning knob, and a transmitter with coils for different frequencies. And there would be a morse key, a set of headphones, and a cot for the quieter moments when the Sparks could catch forty winks between transmissions.

Just like Percy Westerman's youthful character Leslie Dexter, I could imagine myself signing on as the Sparks. The ship would be the *Falaize* (I'd seen the name on the prow of a merchant ship that used to ply between the islands). She would be carrying a mysterious cargo and would be heading for a secret destination. There would be a storm in the South Atlantic and the cargo would break loose in the hold, upsetting the ship's balance. A list would develop and the ship would start taking on water.

There would be dissension among the crew, and even between the ship's officers. The Captain would be loath to call for help, for then the ship's mission might be discovered. The First Officer would support his master but the Second Officer was 'straight up' and knew nothing of the problem cargo they carried.

The Sparks was in a dilemma, struggling between loyalty to his Captain and responsibility for the safety of his brother officers and the below-decks crew. The Captain had taken him aside after they had sailed and had named a small South American port as their destination, but had cautioned him against mentioning it to the remainder of the crew. The exact nature of the cargo he chose not to divulge, although the Sparks suspected it was arms and ammunition for guerrillas operating in the hills of a developing nation.

The *Falaize* was close to thirty years old and was streaked with rust and patches of off-white, blotchy paint where sporadic and inadequate efforts had been made to 'spruce up the old girl.' His wireless cabin was an 8 ft by 9 ft low-ceilinged structure immediately aft of the funnel, placed there as if it had been an afterthought. Inside, its walls were covered with operating charts, wireless frequency warnings, small pointed pins on which he had impaled messages, and large pegs on which hung his sou'wester and winter clothing. Behind his chair was a bench-type seat that served double-duty as a makeshift bed for brief rest periods during emergencies when he had to maintain continuous watch in the wireless cabin.

Such an emergency existed now. The cabin had a twenty-degree list, which caused his pipe and ashtray to slide off the table and crash to the floor, joining the coffee mug, pencils, and erasers that had preceded them with each successive roll of the plunging ship.

He made no attempt to retrieve them. His right hand clutched a black knob on the receiver, which he swept slowly back and forth over a circular dial. The palm of his left hand pressed a headphone firmly against his left ear as he tried to tune in a distant weather report. He was hardly aware of the Second Officer's abrupt entry.

In quick succession, the cabin door was flung open, the ship gave a particularly vicious lurch, and the Second Officer was propelled violently into the little room, accompanied by a deluge of whipped spray that spattered droplets onto the Sparks's logbook and over the map on the opposite wall.

'Sorry!' the Second Officer spluttered, snapping the door shut by pushing firmly on it with his buttocks. He lifted the hood of his sou'wester backward off his head. 'I would have brought you a hot toddy,' he continued, steadying himself against a bulkhead, 'but the galley is flooded, the cook has broken his arm, and I'd've never got it across the deck.'

'It's pretty serious,' the Sparks agreed, then raised the palm of his hand vertically to silence his visitor while he wrote a message being transmitted by a passenger liner, the morse code letters almost indistinguishable above the crackling of static. 'It's the *Leeuwarden*,' he translated. 'She's reporting winds gusting up to ninety knots.'

'Where is she?'

'Two hundred miles south.'

The Second Officer couldn't help displaying his concern: 'That's where we're headed! Have you asked her to stand by, in case we need assistance?'

'Not yet. The Skipper said to wait.'

'Wait! For what, for God's sake?'

He shrugged. There was nothing he could say.

'Does the Skipper know about the weather up ahead?'

The Sparks said he thought not. He hadn't had much chance to talk to the Skipper.

'Then you had better tell him!' the Second Officer shouted, pulling the hood of his sou'wester forward over his head. He waited for the ship to roll toward the door, opened it quickly, and in one quick movement stepped over the transom and was gone. The door slammed shut behind him, in concert with the return roll of the ship. This time his adroit manoeuvres prevented any water from sloshing into the cabin.

The Sparks stumbled across to the speaking tube, lifted out the plug, and called into it. The tube fed directly up to the bridge thirty yards ahead, but there was no response. He called again, then placed his right ear against the end of the tube. All he could hear was a splash and gurgle. Somehow, sea water had got into it.

There was no alternative but to go up to the bridge himself. He grabbed his black sou'wester from its peg and, steadying himself against the table, waited while the old tub shuddered in response to a particularly heavy wave, then pulled the slick, heavy clothing over his head.

Just as the Second Officer had done, he waited until the ship seemed to be roughly on an even keel as it rolled from one extremity to the other. At that precise moment he swung open the door, stepped smartly over the transom, and slammed the door shut behind him.

Immediately the wind tugged and sucked at his sou'wester, threatening to pull him to the rail. He grabbed the rope that had been lashed at hip height along the length of the deck, to prevent crew members from being washed overboard by the tumultuous waves that kept tumbling over the ship's side. Waves that left a knee-high, frothing maelstrom of water racing toward the scuppers; water that grabbed so fiercely at his legs that it threatened to pull him face down onto the deck.

He stood still for a full minute, or as still as the bucking ship and grasping wind and water would allow, waiting for his eyes to become accustomed to the dark. The shrieking wind and crashing waves assaulted his ears almost as fiercely as they assaulted his body. High above him he could glimpse the mast lights swinging in wide, erratic arcs.

In the fleeting moments when the deck was momentarily free of water, he inched his way forward toward the bridge, first hauling on the rope and then pausing and hanging on for dear life as the ship rolled in the other direction and dug its scuppers deep into the water, the frothing brine swirling almost knee-deep around him. His fingers were already numb with cold, and he found it difficult to breathe properly as the gale-force winds whipped spume into his face.

He had progressed no more than ten feet—in what seemed like fifteen minutes but was more likely only one or two—when a particularly vicious wave pushed the bow high in the air. The old *Falaize* shuddered, paused momentarily, then, as an enormous wave passed beneath its creaking hull, swung forward in a steeply descending dive. Water hurled itself at the Sparks almost up to his armpits. It pulled his feet from under him and prised his fingers from the rope. He felt himself sliding helplessly toward the combing. Just then the ship's klaxon horn gave a long, loud blast….

I jumped at the sudden intrusion into my thoughts. Turning around, I saw that the *St Julien*—my favourite of all the mailboats—had nosed into the harbour and was sidling in toward the quay behind me, on the other side of the jetty, announcing her presence to the town of St Peter Port with a long blast of her horn.

*

On some mornings I chose to watch the mailboats arrive and depart from Castle Cornet, on the other side of the harbour. I would turn right at the foot of Smith Street and run in the opposite direction, down High Street, past the Town Church, and south along the Esplanade. The harbour was shaped like the claws of a giant crab, with the granite walls that formed the large ends of the claws reaching inward at the extremities to within 150 yards of one another, a lighthouse at each tip. Between the claws was a calm, safe harbour for the multitude of small boats that frequented the island.

Castle Cornet in 1928, with shipping signal mast.
(The mast was demolished during the German occupation.)
Photo: Carel Toms

Castle Cornet was adjacent to the southern promontory. I had read in an ancient document in the Guilles-Alles Library that the original parts of the castle were more than seven hundred years old, the earliest buildings and battlements having been erected in 1206. Many additions had been made in succeeding years, and by 1670 the upper reaches were capped by an impressive round tower known as a donjon, or keep.

One incident in the castle's history particularly captured my imagination. Near midnight on 29th December 1672, lightning struck the powder magazine and the resulting explosion blew apart the area known as The Citadel, levelling the upper buildings. But…

> …the Right Honorable Lord Hatton (the governor), being at the Time of the blowing up of the Magazine afast asleep, happened to be blown upon the Battlments of a Wall in his Bed, and was not awakened but by a Shower of Hail that fell upon his Face and made him sencible where he was. A most miraculous preservation indeed, worthy to be admired for the House was all blown over the Walls and razed to the very ground, nothing of it being left standing but the outward Door case. *

My amusement on reading this account, however, was mitigated by the very next paragraph, for it told of

- Extracts (c. 1673) from a Dobree Manuscript from *Transactions Sociètè Guernesiaise*, 1930.

the death of the governor's wife, mother, two of his daughters, and a children's nurse. The governor's two infant children, however, one of whom the nurse was holding in her arms when the explosion occurred, escaped unharmed.

I entered the castle through a dark, arched tunnel with, at each end, the prongs of a heavy cast-iron gate hanging from inside an inverted channel carved deep into the granite roof. I walked quickly then, for fear the gate might suddenly be lowered (though I knew intuitively that the mechanism probably was rusted out and wouldn't work).

When the gate was lowered, I mused, *the castle must have been almost impregnable.*

This was the only way to enter the castle. The vertical walls on all sides would have prevented invasion from the island or the sea.

I chased through a maze of winding, low-ceilinged, narrow passages set between granite walls, and up countless steps of worn stone to the rebuilt Citadel. I half walked and half ran, as quickly as my chubby legs would allow, fearful that I might be too late.

As I emerged onto the top of the Citadel I took a quick look at the signals already on the masts. The black drum between the first and second yardarms I had expected to see, since it reported that the Southern Railways mailboat had already docked in the harbour. I was more interested in the Great Western Railways house flag; it was still below the lowest yardarm and there was still no flag at the top of the mast. Good! The GWR mailboat had not yet been sighted.

Part of Prisoners' Walk, Castle Cornet.
Photo by the author

The lookout was a small, octagon-shaped wood structure half buried in an earth bank, with seven horizontal windows each about 15 inches high set into the upper half of its eight sides. A slim door was set into the eighth side, and I stumbled down five stone steps cut into the grass bank to reach it. I knocked gently and almost immediately a gruff voice invited me to enter.

The lookout post was manned by a retired sea captain, or so he had seemed to imply during my previous visits. He was stocky, about 5 ft 4 in., age about 70, and dressed in heavy black rubber boots, baggy black corduroy trousers, and a thick hand-knitted navy blue sweater made with oiled wool and known locally as a Guernsey. His hair was grey but still thick, almost shaggy. In fact, the 'captain' epitomized my image of the sea-faring man signed on by Captain Smollett and Squire Trelawney, as second-in-command of the schooner *Hispaniola* at the start of their search for Treasure Island.

The octagonal shack was lined vertically with long grey-white laths running from the floor to the base of the look-out windows. In the centre of the seven-foot-wide area stood a wooden pedestal with, on its top, a telescope supported by a freely rotating joint. Five inches beneath the telescope lay a flat, circular compass rose, about 24 inches in diameter, with the 360 degrees of the compass etched into its surface at two-degree intervals.

'Run all the way, did you?' the Captain greeted me laconically.

'Sort of,' I grinned breathlessly.

'What's the hurry, then?' the Captain asked, his eyebrows raised high above his glasses.

'I…er…wanted to get here,' I said. 'It's a sort of race,' I added sheepishly, feeling I ought to explain. 'Between me and the mailboat. I try to get here before you put the cones up.'

I really meant that I hoped the Captain would allow me to haul up the signals. (He'd let me help once before, with both of us pulling on the lanyard.) But I'd been taught never to ask for favours; it was better to earn them.

The Captain lowered his head to the telescope eyepiece and scanned the southeast horizon. I shivered, partly in anticipation and partly because the cool dampness of the lookout post was beginning to filter through my sweaty clothing. There was no heat in the structure, summer or winter, and there was always a breeze—more often a healthy wind—scudding past its exposed position on top of the Citadel.

'I thought you weren't coming back,' the Captain commented, his eye to the telescope. 'You've not been up here for some time.'

'I went to the other side. On the new jetty.'

'You did, did you?' the Captain grunted, his eye still glued to the eyepiece.

It was difficult to explain to the Captain that I had to choose between watching close up as the boats were unloaded and then reloaded, which I preferred, or watching the mailboats from a distance as they eased into and then out of their berths, turned slowly within the harbour outer basin, and then steamed out between the two lighthouses, black smoke pouring from their funnels. To run all the way round to the new jetty after the mailboat arrived—like running all three sides of a 'U'—would have taken too long. And, anyway, I could hardly dessert the Captain as soon as the *St Julien* or *St Helier* or *St Patrick* had been sighted and the flags signifying its arrival had been hauled up onto the mast. It wouldn't be polite.

In the ensuing silence I glanced round the tiny room. Hanging from nails driven into the wooden laths were postcard-size photographs of older mailboats: the *Vera*, which had been a troop-carrier in the war; the *Courier*, which I had once travelled on alone, to Alderney, when I was nine; the *Caesarea*, which had served on the Southampton-Guernsey run; and the little *New Fawn*, which traded between Poole, on England's south coast, Guernsey, and St Malo in France. Beside them were faded snapshots of a burlier, jauntier Captain standing on the bridge of an unnamed ship, and another one of him standing beside a dark-haired woman in a long dress, in front of a garden gate.

On the opposite wall, enclosed within a brown wooden frame and fronted by glass with a single crack across one corner, were printed instructions and illustrations for signalling the sighting and arrival of visiting ships. There were eight drawings, four displaying how to identify a ship arriving from the north, essentially from England, and four showing how to identify a ship arriving from the south, generally from Jersey or St Malo. Each illustration showed a central mast with two cross arms—properly known as yardarms—so that there were in effect three segments for displaying flags and drums.

CODE OF SIGNALS

For Shipping, which are made use of at Castle Cornet and Fort George Signal Stations :

Extremities of the yards projecting upwards mark the North. Extremities of the yards projecting downwards mark the South.

The signals on the upper yard are for square-rigged vessels, viz. :—Ships, barques, or brigs, either under steam or sail. The signals on the lower yards are for fore and aft vessels, viz. :—Brigantines, schooners, and cutters, either under steam or sail.

The Southern Railway's Mail Boat is signalled thus :—

1.—Packet due from Southampton. 2.—Packet still due from Southampton, but a steamer in sight.
3.—Packet from Southampton in sight. 4.—Packet from Southampton in the harbour.
5.—Packet due from Jersey. 6.—Packet still due from Jersey, but a steamer in sight.
7.—Packet from Jersey in sight. 8.—Packet from Jersey in the harbour.

The Weymouth Mail Boat is signalled in a similar manner, with the exception that the G.W.R. Co.'s Flag is used instead of a drum.

Instructions for positioning signal flags and drums on yardarms atop Castle Cornet. (The illustration was found, severely damaged, in a 1932 Guernsey Press Almanac)

The drums were pictured as square dots but in real life were black leather drums about eighteen inches square.

The Captain lifted his head back from the telescope and surveyed me quizzically: 'How old would you be?'

'Twelve. I'm just twelve.'

'Hmmmph!' The Captain peered again into the eyepiece. 'You planning on going to sea?' he asked, without removing his eye from the lens.

'Well, I had sort of thought of it.'

'Tough life, you know.'

'I thought I could be…well…a wireless operator.' I was sharing a confidence I had never offered to anyone.

'A Sparks!' The Captain momentarily lifted his head away from the telescope. 'Right?'

I nodded.

'Still tough.' The Captain looked again into the eyepiece. 'And lonely, too. You mind being on your own?'

'Not really.'

'You can't expect to have a proper home life. Not like ordinary people.'

I didn't know if I was expected to reply, so remained silent.

'Oh, it's not so bad, when you're on board,' he continued. 'You'll be able to handle it, I expect. You can always talk to the ship's crew, when you've not got the headphones on.'

I nodded again.

'But it's tough on them that stays home.' The Captain stood up and jerked a thumb at the photograph of himself and the young woman beside the gate. 'But I don't suppose that'll mean much to you, yet.'

He reached round to the squall jacket hanging from a hook behind him and pulled a weather-beaten, well-chewed pipe and a soft-leather pouch from a side pocket. Unfolding the pouch, he said: 'Here! You keep an eye open for me.' And he beckoned for me to come around to his side of the telescope. 'She'll be coming in on a heading of three-three-two degrees. That's one-five-two from here. About sou'-sou'-east.'

I scrambled around to the proffered eyepiece and pulled it down to my eye level.

The Captain laughed. 'You'll only see birds like that.'

He pushed gently down on the front of the telescope. I stretched upward, keeping my eye against the eyepiece, until I stood on tiptoe. But the telescope still sloped skyward.

'You are a titch, aren't you?' grunted the Captain, taking a slim wooden box from where it stood on end beside the wall and laying it flat on the floor. 'Here! Stand on this.'

I stepped up and levelled the telescope. 'I can see the horizon.' I announced.

'Right! But that way you'll only see the *Joybell* on her way back from Sark. Turn the telescope about twenty degrees to starboard.'

He placed his hands on my shoulders and eased me to the left, so the front of the telescope swung to the right. I shuffled my feet to retain my balance.

'You're about right now.' He said. 'Just search back and forth along the horizon.'

'Easy does it,' he added a few moments later, his fingers deep into his tobacco pouch. 'Search across a small segment of the horizon at a time, and do it *slowly.*'

The Captain lifted a pinch of tobacco between his thumb and two fingers, pushed it into the bowl of his pipe, and tamped it down with almost exaggerated care. He paused to watch, then I sensed him lean over and, with only the slightest pressure, ease the telescope a little farther to the right. Then he dug his free hand into the pouch and pulled out a few more strands of tobacco, which he again carefully tamped down.

'I…I think I can see it,' I gasped. 'A smudge of smoke.'

'Not a funnel?' the Captain asked.

'No. Just smoke.'

'What's the bearing?'

I removed my eye from the eyepiece and looked at the graduated compass rose on the surface of the mount. 'Would it be one-five-five?'

The Captain leaned over. 'Near enough.'

'Is that right, then?'

The Captain peered quizzically at me across the compass rose.

'For the mailboat?' I asked.

'Look again. Check the telescope hasn't moved.'

'The smoke's still there.'

'Then I should imagine that's it.'

I stood back from the telescope. 'Do you want to see for yourself?'

The Captain struck a match and lowered the flame onto the bowl of his pipe.

'No,' he said, between puffs. 'No. I think I can trust your judgment.'

I looked into the telescope again and then back toward the Captain. 'If it is the mailboat, shouldn't you…' I paused. 'I mean, shouldn't there be a signal?'

'Quite right, my boy. What do you suggest?'

'A red pennant, to go right to the top of the mast.'

'Why?'

'Here! It's on the chart.' I pointed to the sixth diagram. 'A red pennant means an unknown ship has been sighted.'

'Why unknown?' the Captain asked laconically. 'After all, it's coming from the right direction.'

'Because it's only a puff of smoke. We haven't seen the funnel yet.'

'Then I think you had better do something about it,' the Captain grunted, and handed me a large rusty key.

'You go on up. I'll bring the telescope.'

I scrambled up the mound on which the mast was anchored and inserted the key into a narrow slot in the door of a white-painted box. The key turned squeakily and then the door sprang open. I pulled out a long red flag with two short lengths of rope extending from above and below it, each tied to a wooden peg.

'Can you find the right lanyard?' the Captain asked.

I sorted through the lengths of rope wound around the cleats at the bottom of the pole. 'This one?' I asked, pulling a rope toward me.

'Next to it, on the left,' the Captain suggested. 'You've got it. Know how to loop it in?'

'You pull the rope down and push these ends in to the loops,' I explained, holding up the two wooden pegs. 'My grandfather has a flagpole. He showed me how.'

I unwound the running cable from around the cleat and pulled the loop of rope through my fingers until the lower loop rested in my hands. Holding the two strands in the palm of one hand, I pushed one of the pegs attached to the red pennant through the loop, like pushing a button through a buttonhole. Then I pulled the second loop toward me and tucked the other peg through it.

'There!' I announced, and I hauled the flag to the top of the mast.

'That's fine,' the Captain agreed, 'but you still need to show where the packet is coming from.' He pointed to a yardarm on which the ends were turned down. 'Get out one of the smaller drums and hang it near the end of that yard.'

From the box I pulled out a twelve-inch drum, tied it to a short rope hanging from the lower yardarm, and hauled it into position so that it hung from just below the down-turned end.

The Captain explained that the down-turned end meant "from the south" and the up-pointed end on the other side of the yardarm meant "from the north." 'That way, no matter from which side you're viewing the mast, the message is the same.'

We sat side by side on the grass, the wind whistling in the ropes above us, causing the pennant to crack like a whip. The Captain aligned the telescope to the southeast and looked toward the approaching smudge, now visible to the naked eye. 'Keep an eye on it,' he said, handing me the telescope. 'Tell me when you know it's the mailboat.'

'When I can read the name?'

'Lord, no! Can't you tell by the shape?'

'Yes, I think so. Single funnel; square rigging. I've watched them come in.'

Five minutes later I knew for sure it was one of the Great Western Railway mailboats.

'What do you do now, then?' the Captain asked.

'Pull the house flag right to the top, in place of the pennant.'

'Right! And what about the small drum?'

'Oh, it stays where it is. Right till she's in the harbour.'

Ten minutes later I lowered the telescope, 'It's the St Patrick,' I said, 'Do I put up her flag?'

'She doesn't have one, other than the house flag. And that's already up.' The Captain looked at me for a moment. 'Do you know what to do next?'

'When she comes in, you mean?'

'Aye.'

'Lower the house flag so it's between the yardarms, like the drum for the Isle of Sark?'

'Aye. And take down the little drum.'

The *St Patrick* had entered the Russell—the body of water between Guernsey and the islands of Herm and Jethou—and was drawing level with Castle Cornet. Beneath the red funnel I could see the three lifeboats on the port side, the brown woodwork of the bridge contrasting sharply with the white painted upperwork beneath it. I could even see passengers standing on the deck, crowded between the lifeboats and on the aft platform. She was starting to turn port now, toward the harbour entrance, the wake behind her making a graceful arc.

I clambered up the earth bank and fingered the lanyards until I found the one holding the house flag. I glanced down to see if I had the Captain's approval, but the old sailor was watching the *St Patrick* as she reduced speed, his pipe clenched between his teeth. The passengers were clearly visible now, and I could see a ship's officer leaning out of the side window of the bridge staring toward me. I slowly unwound the rope from around the cleat.

'Always keep the cable from a mast arm running through the palms of your hands,' the Captain called. 'If there's a strong wind, and it whips the cable away from you, you're in trouble. With a cone or ball, the weight might be enough to hold the rope down as it drops. But with a flag up the mast, it'll just stream in the wind. You'll not recover the ropes until the wind drops.'

The *St Patrick* was nosing in now, had drawn level between the lighthouses at the ends of the two piers.

'Now?' I asked.

'Now!' the Captain repeated. And he laughed.

I laughed too and hauled down on one rope and let the other slide through my hand. When the flag dropped into the middle segment, between the two yardarms, I drew the ropes together and lashed them in a series of S's around the cleat.

'Now for the drum,' I muttered to myself, turning to the rope leading to the end of the downward-turned

The St Julien steams into Guernsey harbour on an unusually calm day.

yardarm. I unwrapped the rope from around the cleat, let the weight of the drum run the rope through my fingers, pulled the drum in toward me, and pushed the wooden pegs out of the loops. Then I retied the pair of ropes around the cleat and pushed the drum into the storage box.

'Now everyone knows both mailboats are in,' the Captain announced, though we both knew it, 'and bring the key with you. Let's get out of this wind. I've got some cocoa in my thermos.'

*

There is no lookout post on Castle Cornet now, for in 1941 the German occupying force levelled the Citadel atop the castle and poured tons of reinforced concrete to provide a concealed bunker in its place. Neither is there a signal mast: it was removed at the same time and was never replaced after Guernsey was liberated. By then radio communication had done away with the need for manual signals. And with it a segment of my life; a segment etched into my memory, but which sadly will never be experienced by today's Guernsey youths.

6

First Interview

July 1938, and my first real interview. For the occasion my mother had at last conceded she should buy me a pair of long trousers. I was thankful because they concealed my knees, even though the grey flannel made them itch.

The Headmaster invited me to sit on a hard, polished upright chair beside his desk, so we could talk to each other across the corner. But, in my nervousness, instead of settling well back into the chair I perched hesitantly on its front edge. We had not progressed far into the interview before I could feel the wooden edge cutting a crease into my buttocks. It was extremely uncomfortable, yet I was far too nervous to push myself further back; to make what I sensed would be an undignified move.

The Reverend Doctor Francis Hardy was old and thin, almost frail. He had silver-grey hair and small, gold wire-rimmed glasses that hung low on a long, beaky nose. He wore a black gown over a charcoal-coloured suit and had a white 'dog collar' around his neck, to show that although he was a Headmaster he also was a Man of The Church. I thought perhaps he had just come from holding a service, like matins or communion. No one had thought to tell me that teachers at Elizabeth college wore their black gowns all the time, like a uniform.

The Headmaster's study was spacious, with three tall, almost ceiling-high multi-pane sash windows separated by shelves of ancient books stacked higher than even the Headmaster could reach. Through the middle window, barely noticeable behind the leafy chestnuts that bordered the college grounds, I could make out the round, sand-coloured steeple of St James' Church, where I had been Christened thirteen years earlier.

Do I call him 'Headmaster' or 'Principal'? I thought. The door had HEADMASTER printed on it in faded gold letters, and my grandfather—who once had been a teacher at the Boys Intermediate—called him that. But my parents always referred to him as 'The Principal.' *I'd better stick to 'Sir'*.

The Headmaster lifted his eyes from the folder he had been reading and suddenly erupted into speech: 'Well!' he said, 'tell me why you want to be a pupil at Elizabeth College.'

'Yes, sir.' I had been warned to expect such a question. (I had been prompted by my grandfather to keep silent about the real reason: that my father could afford to pay for only two boys to attend Elizabeth College. If I could win a scholarship it would open the door for both of my brothers.) 'If I am to enter the Civil Service, or go on to a university,' I said, 'I'll need a *proper* education, which I can't get anywhere else in Guernsey.'

The Headmaster 'hurrumphed' in a way that seemed to imply I knew the answer too well.

'You don't think you could do as well by staying on at the Intermediate?' He looked down at some papers on his desk. 'That is where you are now, is it not?'

'Yes, sir,' I replied, but before I could answer the first part of the question the Headmaster asked another.

'I see you went to the Froebel, too. Hmmmm. Which did you like the better?'

'Oh, the Intermediate, sir. It's a *boy's* school.'

It was not strictly true that I preferred the Intermediate, but I sensed it was the expected answer.

The Froebel was almost like a nursery school, run by two middle-aged ladies known to the children as Barney and Willie (their real names were Miss Barnes and Miss Wilson). I had started there when I was five and stayed for six years, cosseted in a warm blanket of gentle persuasion and understanding among a student body in which girls outnumbered boys by more than two to one and the toughest sport was field hockey played by a team of mixed sexes.

Froebel principles may have been sound but they were poor preparation for the male jocularity, ragging, and strict discipline I had to face when, at the age of eleven, I was transferred to the rough, competitive, sports-oriented world of an all-boys school.

'Yes,' the Headmaster murmured, peering at the papers in front of him. 'I see.' He dragged out the last word, like a hiss.

I recognized my own scrawly handwriting. It must be the entrance examination I had written at the college three weeks ago; I and another boy called Davis, also from the Intermediate.

'Your English is good…composition and grammar. Arithmetic? Hmmmm. Passable, I suppose…' He glanced sideways at me, through the corners of his round spectacles. 'Were you coached?'

'I was given extra teaching, sir.' I had been told to admit it.

'By whom?'

'My grandfather, sir. Captain Steele. He's retired now. And Mr Williams, at the Intermediate.'

'Hmmmm. I know of them.' The Headmaster slid the pages together, one above the other flat on his desk. 'Do you know what a scholarship is?'

'I think it means that Elizabeth College will pay for me to come here.'

'Not the College, boy. No. The money comes from philanthropic individuals who have made bequests to the College, to set up scholarships. They will be paying for your schooling. But not your uniform: your parents will have to look after that.'

'Yes, sir.'

'You realize, do you, that we expect more from our scholars than we do from fee-paying pupils?'

'Yes, sir. I do.' My grandfather had made sure I knew that.

'You have to *excel*.' The Headmaster stressed the word, dragged it out sibilantly.

'Yes, sir.'

'Do you excel at sports?'

'Sir?'

'Are you good at sports?'

An awkward question. I was a bit of a duffer at sports, much to my father's disappointment, I suspected. My father was good at sports and had been selected more than once to be on the soccer team that played for the Muratti Cup against Jersey. He had started his newspaper career as a sports reporter.

I had never told anyone, but I had an incipient fear of falling, or being hit by an approaching ball or another team player. I supposed that was why I was no good at contact sports like rugby or football. Anyway, no one ever picked me to play on their team.

'I like to swim, sir.' That at least was true.

'Play cricket?'

'A…little.'

'Football?' The Headmaster again peered sideways at me, lowering his head and looking over the upper rims of his glasses.

'I can manage, sir.'

'Any other accomplishments?'

'I like to play chess.' I was a fair player, but I didn't want to sound as though I was bragging. 'And I collect stamps.'

'Ah! Philately!' The Headmaster seemed to look down his nose at that. 'The College has an active chess club. We need new blood.'

I said I would like to join, but he was already switching to another topic.

'Do you debate?' he asked.

'Sir?'

'Do you like to take part in debates?'

I wasn't sure what he was asking me, and he could see it.

'We have a debating club. Pupils take opposite sides—offer opposite points of view—about a particular topic; try to convince the other side that their point of view is the better.'

'Oh. I see.' I had only a vague idea what he meant, but felt I still should respond. 'Every year I take part in the eisteddfod; recite a long piece, a poem usually.'

'Successfully?'

'Well, yes. I mean, I've won first place twice and second place once.'

'Hmmph.'

I couldn't tell whether he viewed that as something he was pleased to hear. Then he abruptly changed the subject. I found his tactics disconcerting.

'Have you thought of going into The Church?'

I said I had not really considered it. I was trying to say 'no' politely, in deference to the Headmaster's collar.

'When Queen Elizabeth granted a Royal Charter to establish Elizabeth College—that was in 1563—it was with the express intention that the College should provide education for boys wishing to enter The Church. Not so often observed now.' He gave me another sideways glance. 'If not The Church, what then?'

'I…er…I think I'd like to go to sea, sir.'

'Aha!' he exclaimed, apparently well pleased. 'You want to join the Royal Navy.'

No, that's not true. What I really want to be is a wireless operator on a tramp steamer.

But I said out loud: 'Yes, I might like that.' It was too hard to explain.

Again the Headmaster jumped to another topic without warning: 'Do you have any brothers?'

Elizabeth College, illustrated by J Harwood, London, in July 1846. The fields and trees are not set in as spacious grounds as the illustration seems to depict. Permission to reprint courteously granted by Elizabeth College.

'Yes, sir. Two. They're eleven and seven.' I had been told to expand on my answers, just slightly, not to answer in monosyllables.

'And they will be coming to the College?'

'Yes, sir. I expect so.' That was the whole idea of my sitting for the scholarship. My mother and grandmother had also made that clear.

'Will they be coming here in September?'

'Just one, Sir. My next brother: Anthony.'

The Headmaster lifted up my examination papers and arranged them neatly on one side of his desk. 'There,' he said. 'I think that's all I need to know. Your parents will be getting a letter from the Board, informing them whether or not you have been accepted. That will be all for now.'

He waved vaguely toward the door.

I said 'Thank you, sir,' slid off the chair, and tiptoed out. My shoes apologized for their newness as I squeaked across the room.

Is that all? I thought. *If he was really serious about me, wouldn't he have asked a lot more questions?*

I sauntered slowly out of the College and down the Grange toward Smith Street and my father's office. I was convinced that my ten minutes with the Headmaster was as near as I was likely to come to entering the College gates in September. And how was I going to explain *that* to my parents?

But I worried needlessly, for two weeks later both Davis's and my parents received letters announcing we had been awarded scholarships. The letters pointedly described the criteria affecting our presence at Elizabeth College (mostly, that we were expected to contribute “above average” performance), and listed the clothes and equipment they would need to purchase for us before we made our presence known on our first day of school in September.

*

Yes. There was no doubt about it: I liked Elizabeth College far better than the Boys Intermediate. And now the Froebel remained just a childhood memory. Compared to other boys of my age I still tended to be unassertive, unready for the rougher jostling, even though a lot of the ‘softness’ I had carried with me from the Froebel had been erased during the preceding two years.

To my surprise, unexpected capabilities sprung to the fore which helped establish me not entirely as a duffer. Academically, because of the extra tutoring I had received, I stood up well in the initial weeks, during the important first few days when value judgments were made by teachers and pupils alike. For sports I elected swimming, which was available at the outdoor seawater pool at la Valette in September and early October, and again in May, June, and July. Other pupils rated me highly for my imperviousness to the chilly water and propensity for long-distance swimming, although my teachers threw reproachful glances at me because often I was tardy in returning to class.

La Valette was close to Castle Cornet, beyond the South Esplanade and the inner harbour, and the boys had to run to and from the pool. Getting there was easy, downhill all the way. But my tendency to be last out of the pool and my dreamy slowness in drying and dressing meant I was also last in the stream of moist-haired boys panting up Constitution Steps and the steep slope of Sausmarez Street, wet bathing suits rolled in damp towels tucked under their arms.

There were a few features of College life that delighted me, some that amused me, and one or two that distressed me. I loved the first day of a new term. The night before my mother would lay out my clothes—all new, chosen and tried on at the Pioneer in High Street: *long* grey flannel trousers and suit jacket, white shirt, white undervest and underpants, black tie and socks, and black shoes. And on the top, like the dot above an 'i', my school cap, blue with white piping. I would plop it on my head while still in my pyjamas, and wear it while I pulled on my underwear, socks, shirt, and trousers.

Unlike the Intermediate, which required that its pupils wear their school caps only when they were attending school or school-related functions, the College demanded that its pupils wear their caps *at all times* when they were outside, even when they were not wearing their school uniform. If, of an evening, I cycled to la Villiaze to watch the Royal Air Force Ansons flying in and out of the airport, or along Fort Road to go swimming at Fermaine Bay, I had to remember to wear my cap. Should I meet one of the teachers—or, for that matter, any adult whom I knew—I was expected to greet the person by grasping the peak of my cap with one hand and lifting the cap two or three inches above my head, simultaneously saying 'Good afternoon' or 'Good evening' and adding the person's name, or 'Sir' if it was a teacher. Failure to make the greeting courteously, or to be seen without a cap, meant I would be reported and punished the following day. Most often, the punishment was to write one hundred lines (in my case, "*I will return to the College from La Vallette on time*").

Caning still existed, but at the College it was more clearly identified as a punishment and applied less indiscriminately than had been the case at the Intermediate.

I enjoyed belonging to the chess club, although I moved pieces more by intuition than with skill. I also discovered in carpentry class that I was more capable in working with wood than I expected, and was selected to help build sets for the College's Spring production of Gilbert and Sullivan's operetta *Iolanthe.* Later I became part of the behind-scenes production crew, thankful that my voice was 'breaking,' which prevented me from being chosen to be one of the fairies on stage, as was happening to other boys of my size.

Classed as 'hopeless' at cricket and football, I tried grass hockey with only moderate success, still limited by my lack of speed and assertiveness. Gym classes, too, became a problem that I had not anticipated. When the gym master told the boys to scale the thick ropes hanging from heavy S-hooks screwed into the ceiling, I was assailed by an incipient fear that my arms might not carry my weight and I would plunge fifteen feet to the hardwood floor. So I would pretend I was 'having difficulty' in gripping the ropes with my knees, and my clowning antics with my legs flailing about as they tried to grasp the elusive rope became renowned among the Third Form boys.

When our rope climbing skills were to be tested about three weeks before the end of my first year, I 'slipped and fell' as I ran up the steps to the gym from the changing room and 'twisted my ankle.' As I had to remember to limp at home as well as at school, my mother insisted I see the family doctor, who suspected a greenstick fracture and wrote a note excusing me from gym classes for the rest of that term. I was ashamed that I had allowed myself to be caught up in a deceit that I could not correct, and felt different from the other boys because they jumped and climbed with ease. And I felt lonely because there was no one to whom I could confide my distress.

I did not know then that another boy was experiencing similar problems at Birkhamstead School, some twenty miles northwest of London. Thirty-three years later, Graham Greene would write in his autobiography:

> The only class I actively hated was held in the gym. I was very bad at gymnastics…I particularly disliked trying to vault or climb a rope or scramble on the parallel bars, and I pretended, whenever that class came around, that I was ill. I would walk up onto the Common and stay there, hidden among the gorse bushes with their yellow flowers until school was over. *

* Graham Greene, *A Sort of Life* (New York: Simon and Schuster, 1971), p. 65, 67, 68.

7

Schoolboy Soldier

Before I entered Elizabeth College I knew I would have to join the O.T.C.: the Officers Training Corps. My mother and grandmother *expected* me to carry on the Steele's military tradition. (My grandfather had had a stroke the previous summer and died without knowing that his coaching helped his first grandson win a seat to the College.) So I never questioned whether I *wanted* to join—I just signed up. My father, who had more recent and more vivid memories of trench warfare, and was badly wounded at Rues Vertes in November 1917, seemed less enthusiastic. Yet he made no attempt to dissuade me.

The O.T.C. was a part-time cadet corps designed to give College boys elementary military training and—as its name implied—offer experience that would accelerate their promotion if they chose to make a career in the Services. It would certainly provide an edge for boys competing for a position at one of the military colleges. The Corps met twice a week after school at the armoury on Arsenal Road, and occasionally for special exercises on Saturdays. Senior boys also attended a training camp on the mainland during the summer holidays, and that was something I really looked forward to.

To my mild surprise I fell easily into the military routine. True, the drills and marching were boring and I did not particularly appreciate being shouted at by Major Caldwell, but the discipline and the need to conform seemed to agree with me. (Major Caldwell was really one of the College masters, but his Army experience before joining the College allowed him to carry his rank with him.) I even enjoyed cleaning my uniform buttons with Brasso, buttonstick, and brush, and polishing my boots to a sharp, reflective shine. And cleaning both the inside and outside of a Lee-Enfield rifle seemed less onerous than I had expected.

The cadets' uniforms were of the type worn in the 1914-1918 war, complete with plus-four style trousers and puttees, the latter like long khaki bandages that were wound around each leg from ankle to knee. When the layers were neatly overlapped, their wearers looked smart on parade. But in practical exercises, when I had to run across L'Ancresse Common and crawl over the sand dunes or pull myself along on my elbows through long spiky grass, the puttees slipped and bunched around my ankles. Or, worse, they unwound and tripped me as I ran.

It was at the firing range on L'Ancresse Common that I faced my greatest trauma, yet surprisingly enhanced my reputation. The boys were instructed to lie on their stomachs six at a time, facing the targets with their bodies angled about fifteen degrees to the left and their legs spread apart. In front of each boy lay a rifle resting on two sandbags, with the muzzle pointing toward the targets and the bolt pulled back. Fifty yards ahead of them were six bullseye targets, each about eight inches in diameter, pinned against a sackcloth frame with a high sandbank behind it. A red flag, hauled to the top of a short pole stuck into the sand, waved stiffly in the northwest breeze blowing from L'Ancresse Bay.

'As long as that red flag is up, you don't even *think* of touching your rifle,' Major Caldwell shouted, standing at the far left and slightly ahead of the row of reclining figures.

When the red flag was lowered, he told us, we were to pick up our rifles, rest our left forearm on the sandbags, and wedge the butt of the rifle into the right shoulder. We were then to rest the right cheek against the polished wood of the rifle butt, adjust the rear sight above the barrel for a distance of fifty yards, then use our right eye to align the sights so that the whole target rested in the concave cup of the rear sight and the centre of the bullseye was at the upper tip of the front sight.

'When you have achieved that condition,' Major Caldwell bellowed, 'close the bolt, release the safety catch with your thumb, resight the target, hold your breath, and sque-e-e-eze—*don't pull*—the trigger.'

Click! Click! Click-click-click! Click!

'All right! Now pull back the bolt.'

There were six almost simultaneous click-chops.

'I'll be bringing each of you five rounds of ammunition,' he shouted. 'You are not to touch them until I tell you to. Is that understood?'

I raised my right hand in acknowledgment, in unison with the five other boys. From my position at the end of the line, I could see Major Caldwell's khaki-clad figure stride from behind each boy and place five rounds of ammunition on the grass beside the boy's right elbow.

I stared at the five lethal-looking rounds placed beside me. Each was about two-and-a-half inches long and one-quarter of an inch in diameter. The back half was made of brass and had a lip around the end to prevent it from sliding up the breech when the bullet was fired. There was an indentation in the blunt end, which I presumed was where the firing pin hit and caused the explosion that ejected the bullet. The bullet itself was the front half, all shiny silver-grey metal that curved to a point.

Major Caldwell called for the red flag to be lowered.

'Now!' he shouted from behind us. 'Insert one round at a time. Close the bolt. Release the safety catch. Then fire when ready!'

Chop-click, the rifle went as I slid a bullet into place and pushed the bolt forward. A moment later there was an explosion from the other end of the line, and then from the rifle beside me. I pushed the rifle butt firmly into my right shoulder and looked along the sights: they stood out clearly, but the target beyond them was only a blur. Judging the smudge of black to be the centre of the target, I squeezed the trigger. The rifle kicked back with a resounding jolt that hurt my shoulder, and the loudness of the explosion set up a ringing in my right ear. Four more times I inserted a round, sought for the centre of the target, and felt the rifle butt bite into my shoulder. Then I raised my right arm to indicate I had finished firing.

'Check that the bolt is open,' the major bellowed. 'Leave your rifles on the ground and stand up behind them.' He waited until all six boys were standing and then signalled to another khaki-clad youth to raise the red flag. 'Now walk down to your target, unpin it, and put this one up in its place.'

He walked down the line and handed each boy a fresh target. 'Bring your target back to me,' he shouted after us.

From thirty feet away I could see that my target was unpunctured: I had not hit it even once! Beside me I could hear the shouts of the five other boys: 'I've got three!'; 'Cor, look at that!'; 'Look, a bullseye!'

I examined the edges of my target to see if there might be a nick, perhaps. There was none. Disconsolate, I walked back to the firing line, not bothering to take the target down.

'It's not how many bullseyes you get that's important,' the major was saying to the boys gathered round him, 'but how you group your shots. A group shows that you have been consistently accurate. When you know how far the centre of your group is from the bullseye, then you can offset the centre of the target the next time you shoot.'

He wrote each boy's name on his target as he examined it. 'Not bad, Mahy; a little scattered,' he said to one. And to another: 'Rather random, Smythe. You're allowing the rifle to swing about too much.'

He looked at me: 'Let me see yours.'

'None, sir. It's blank.'

'None? Let me see.' The major held out his hand.

'I didn't take it down, sir. It's still up.'

The major lifted his field glasses to his eyes and peered toward the target. The five other boys were silent, intrigued, a little embarrassed for the poor sod who had missed entirely, yet relieved it hadn't happened to them.

'By gad, you're right. Are you sure you were firing at the correct target?'

I nodded.

The major turned to the five other boys: 'Does anyone have more than five bullet holes?'

No one had.

'Are you sure you set the sights correctly?'

I nodded again, but the major still walked over to the rifle at the end of the line, picked it up, and peered at the sites.

'No. It's all right,' he muttered. He turned and looked quizzically at me, sensing my despondence. 'Try again,' he said encouragingly.

He turned toward the others. 'Everyone ten feet back!' he commanded, and then he called to the flag bearer to take down the red flag.

He studied my movements as I settled myself onto the ground, picked up the rifle, pulled it in to my shoulder, and rested my forearms on the sandbags. 'Go through the motions, just as if you had a round up the spout. I want to see what you might be doing wrong.'

I slid the bolt forward and snapped it down, aligned the blurred target as best I could, squeezed the trigger, and heard the click as the firing pin shot forward into the empty chamber.

'Looks fine,' the major said, and placed five rounds on the grass beside the sandbags.

Instead of picking them up, I lowered the rifle and rolled onto my side. 'I…I really can't see the target properly,' I said, admitting something I had never told anyone before.

'Can't see it? What do you mean?'

'My right eye, sir. It's not very good.' Then I added hastily: 'My left eye's very good, better than most.'

The major pondered for a moment. 'Do you want to use your left eye?'

'I could try, sir.'

'You'll have to lie the other way. It'll be a bit awkward.'

I stood up and, under the major's direction, lay so that my body was angled fifteen degrees to the right instead of to the left.

'Hold the rifle with your right hand and squeeze the trigger with your left,' the major cautioned.

Because I was right-handed the position felt cumbersome, but not impossible.

'Does that pose a problem?'

'No, sir.'

'Then try it. You'll find it a little awkward pulling the bolt back, because it's on the wrong side of the rifle.'

I tried the manoeuvre twice.

'I can manage,' I said.

I felt self-conscious, lying alone on the firing line with all the other cadets watching my every move. *Would I again produce a clean target?* I moaned inwardly. *Would they all see what a duffer I really was?*

'Just take your time, lad,' the Major said, as though he could sense my anguish. 'Don't feel you have to rush.'

He shouted for the red flag to be lowered.

With my left hand I fumbled a cartridge into the chamber and closed the bolt. Then I raised the rifle to my left shoulder, rested my left cheek against the butt, and looked along the sights. This time the back sight was a little blurred because of its nearness to my good eye, but the front sight and the target were crystal clear. Pushing gently onto the sandbags with my forearms, I waited until the target steadied at the tip of the foresight before squeezing the trigger. The now familiar jolt pushed the rifle butt into my left shoulder and set my left ear ringing.

I lowered the rifle and reached awkwardly over it with my left hand, pulled back on the bolt, ejected the spent cartridge, and inserted a fresh one into the slightly smoking chamber. Four times I repeated the procedure and then raised my right arm. Looking back, I noticed the major was watching the target through his field glasses.

'Stand up, then,' the major said, his expression displaying no indication of whether I had hit the target. 'Red flag up, please,' he shouted, and handed me a blank target. 'Go and fetch your target.'

From thirty feet away my good left eye told me that there were blemishes in the lower right quadrant. As I grew closer I saw that I had not once hit the bullseye but I had five holes spaced within about one-and-a-half inches of each other, all in the lower half of the target. Not only had I found the target, but I had managed to make a group. And a smaller group than anyone else!

'That's more like it!' the major congratulated me. 'You'll be fine for single shot firing. We'll have to see what we can do to help you in rapid-fire competition. We'll have you on the Bisley Team, yet!'

I turned away, ostensibly to straighten the rifle which I had lain carelessly at my firing post when I went up to examine the target, but really to conceal the hot flush of embarrassment (and, I had to admit, pleasure) I could feel surging up my neck from under the scratchy uniform collar. There was no way I could let Major Caldwell and the other cadets see that!

*

If I had a long-sighted left eye and a short-sighted right eye, how did I ever manage four years later to pass an extremely stringent eye test and become an air force flyer? Sheer luck! In the intervening years I discovered that, if I blinked my right eye hard when reading the eye chart, a tear would momentarily film over the eye and give me a fleeting moment of perfect vision – just long enough to register the tiny letters on the bottom line of the eye chart in my memory.

Part 3

The Evacuation
June 1940

8

19th June 1940: Morning

Breakfast, which on most days was accompanied by state-of-the-day chitchat, was unusually silent. My brothers had been allowed to sleep longer than usual and still were drowsy, in a mild torpor. My mother, I suspected, was full of questions she could not ask in front of us children, so when she chose to speak she seemed to prattle aimlessly about having to telephone the deputy director of St John Ambulance, where she was the director, to 'make arrangements,' and that she'd have to go to Le Riche's to settle the bill and get food for their sandwiches, and call Mr Mauger to stop delivering milk….

A cautionary glance from her husband stopped her in mid-sentence.

Like my mother, I was bursting with questions but had to remain silent or risk revealing that I had been eavesdropping. Obviously my father was privy to information no one else had heard, and was preoccupied by the enormity of the news he would have to print and the decisions he would have to make.

It was 8:45 when I slid the front wheel of my bike into the angled racks beside the carpentry shop on the north side of Elizabeth College. The youngest boys, my brother Ian among them, played tag in the high walled quadrangle at the rear of the college. The remainder—the bulk of the 227 boys—gathered in groups on the gravelled drive in front of the building or played on the rough grass that led down to the railings facing St James Church.

The sixth-formers, who were the only boys allowed inside the building before the 8:55 bell, were preparing to perform their prefectorial duties. The fifth and fourth-formers—of whom I was one—gathered in small groups on the gravel and discussed chess strategies, news about the evacuation from Dunkirk, and the college's chances of winning the upcoming cricket match against Victoria College in Jersey. The third and second-formers—Tony among them—chased one another among the long, straight hillocks that broke the continuity of the grass beyond the gravelled driveway, their grey knee socks sliding into untidy ridges above their black shoes and their caps slipping sideways over their ears.

The hillocks covered air-raid shelters constructed the previous June. While sabres were being rattled in Western Europe and Neville Chamberlain was declaring peace in our time, the older boys had wielded picks and shovels and cursed the intransigence of the rock-filled soil in front of the college. None of the boys now climbed down the steps or entered the shelters, for to do so was strictly forbidden. They had been allowed into the dank-smelling earth trenches only twice: once when the island's civil defence authorities called a practice air raid drill, and once when an unidentified aircraft had approached from the southeast. Each time they had to feel their way along the damp, dark, narrow corridors, sharp protruding boulders brushing against their knees and hands, and the damp earth muddying the shoulders of their blazers. They were not keen to go back.

Morning assembly was held in the church-like big hall, with arches along the sides and stained-glass windows behind the stage on which the Masters sat. A hymn was sung, the Lesson for the day was read by the duty prefect, The Lord's Prayer was chanted, and a routine warning that the boys were to keep away from the construction going on at the east end of the gym was read by Mr Waite, the Assistant Headmaster. Then the boys filed out, the lines heading toward their regular classrooms accompanied by warnings from the prefects to cut out the talking, just as they did on every day of the school year.

The day seemed so normal that I was glad I had not confided my sparse news to any of the other boys in the Fourth Form, not even to Vernon Collenette. Perhaps I had let my imagination run wild and had inferred too much from the fragmented bits of conversation I had heard.

Mr. Waite was being particularly obnoxious, speaking to the Fourth Form only in French and insisting that the boys reply to him in French. He laced with a barbed tongue those who stumbled.

'Votre accent est atroce!' he lanced at George Luxton, whose father owned the radio shop on Smith Street and was noteworthy for having captured the first television signals to reach Guernsey from England.

'Même pas un patois Guernesiaise? Mais où avez-vous grandi? Montmartre? Plutôt selon moi!' Mr Waite's large stomach shook beneath the folds of the traditional black gown he and all the masters wore, and his short, graying beard, trimmed to a neatly rounded point, seemed to quiver with indignation.

Some of the boys tittered, mainly those who were proficient in French, plus a few who were not but wanted the Master to think they understood.

While Mr Waite's attention was centred on George Luxton, Vernon Collenette passed a miniature chess board to me. My desk was at the right-hand side of the room, against the windows. Vernon Collenette's desk was on my left. The chess board was housed in a slim leather case like a wallet. Inside, the leather had been engraved and shaded to form alternately coloured squares. A slit had been cut horizontally in the lower edge of each square, into which tiny inverted pear-shaped pieces of white card were inserted, each printed with a red or black chess figure. I had been playing this particular game with Collenette for three days, and prided myself that I had been able to keep the game going for so long against such a redoubtable player.

I studied the positions of the remaining pieces, carefully holding the board between my tummy and the edge of the desk so Mr Waite could not see it. If I moved the queen's knight forward I could block Collenette's queen from advancing, and then in the next move I could bring my remaining bishop up and place my opponent's king in check. It might even be checkmate if Collenette moved his own queen diagonally in his next move. But Collenette, I knew from experience, was too strong a player not to have foreseen what I had in mind.

I wished I had Collenette's acute, probing mind, able to think through all possible combinations of moves and predict what my opponent would most likely do next. When I first played against him, I suspected he was not playing his hardest just to keep me in the game, or to give me confidence. More recently I concluded that sometimes I managed to frustrate Collenette's strategies, not because I made particularly clever or intuitive chess moves but because in my innocence I often made unpredictable moves, moves that no experienced player would ever make.

'Est-ce que vous croyez qu'il fait chaud ici?' The Master's sonorous tones interrupted my thoughts.

I looked up: Waite was staring directly at me. Immediately I feared he had spotted the unlawful object in my hand.

'Pardon, monsieur?'

'Il fait chaud ici. Ne croyez-vous pas?'

Whew! I understood 'chaud' all right. The old man must be asking if the room was too warm; or the day outside.

'Oui, monsieur,' I replied truthfully, for with the possibility of imminent exposure the room had suddenly become unbearably warm. 'Il fait très chaud.'

'Alors, je vous ordonne d'ouvrir la fenêtre.'

Ouvrir la fenêtre?, I thought. *Open the window! Everybody knows that!*

'Oui, monsieur.'

As I rose I kept my right hand—the hand farthest away from Waite—below the level of the desk top. In it I held the chessboard, which I silently snapped shut and allowed to slide onto the chair seat.

I turned to the tall sash window above my desk, unwound the rope from its cleat, and let the rope slide between my palms. The heavy upper window slid about two feet down within its wooden gliders. A quick glance behind me showed that Waite was now engaged in a whispered conversation with a sixth form prefect who had entered from the far end of the room. I rewound the rope around its cleat and skittered back to my desk, slipping the chessboard into my pocket.

The prefect handed Waite a slip of folded paper. The Master reached for the pince-nez on his desk and slipped them onto the bridge of his nose. The 17 boys watched in silence as he read the note and said something *sotto voce* to the prefect—who nodded in agreement and tiptoed out of the room. The Master meticulously folded the paper twice, checked that the sides were exactly of equal length, and slid it into a pocket concealed within the folds of his gown.

'Merci, Maitre Blicq' he acknowledged, inclining his head toward the open window and nodding cursorily toward me.

'Cette leçon se terminera plus tôt,' he announced to the class. 'À dix heures quarante-cinq, il y aura une pèriode de récréation de quinze minutes pour que vous puissiez jouer à l'extèrieur. Cette pèriode sera surveillée par les préets, et suivie du'une réunion speċciale à onze heures.'

Waite looked around the room. 'Vous comprenez?' he asked, his bushy grey eyebrows raised high above his pince-nez.

Seeing smiles on some faces and blank looks on others, he repeated his instructions, this time in English, slowly elucidating the words: 'You will go outside at a quarter to eleven for a play period, and then you will come in at eleven o'clock for a special assembly.'

It was ten minutes after eleven before the Headmaster—the Reverend William Henry Goodenough Milnes—strode down the aisle between the rows of seated boys, his black gown trailing behind him. The buzz of chatter was silenced as the boys dutifully rose to their feet, chairs scraping on the polished wood floor. He stepped nimbly up onto the platform and turned to face his school, his gown swinging behind him.

'You may sit,' he announced, and waited for the shuffling, murmuring, and scraping of chairs to cease.

'Your parents will read in today's newspaper—and I am to tell you now—that in a few hours all military forces are to be withdrawn from Guernsey. The Prime Minister, Mr Winston Churchill, has declared that the island is to become undefended territory, as will Jersey and all the smaller Channel Islands.

'This is being done because the German army is less than twenty miles away on the Normandy coast, and the German fighters and bombers will be operating from airfields only a short distance from the island. It would be very difficult—if not impossible—for the Royal Navy and Royal Air Force to defend the island from the mainland.' He referred briefly to more notes held in his hand, and read from them: ' "The British

Government feels that any attempt to defend the islands will result in very high casualties among the islanders. The Government is unwilling to place so many lives in jeopardy''.' He let his eyes scan the long hall. Most of the boys he knew by name, even though he had been Headmaster of Elizabeth College for only ten months. To the youngest at the front his words probably had only minor impact, and it would need more explanation by their room Masters and parents before they fully understood the implications of the impending event he was describing. He would not want to have to make the decision their parents must make today: Were they to keep their sons and daughters here, in what inevitably would become Nazi-occupied territory? Or were they to send them away to England across enemy-controlled waters. And for how long? The war could go on for years. The last one had.

The boys in the middle—the 10 to 15 year olds—watched him intently. They understood what he was saying but did not fully comprehend the implications.

The older boys—the prefects and seniors, whom he knew best—had already been told what had to be done. In less than a year many would be in uniform. He knew they looked forward to the day they could serve their country, but he also knew what that meant, and he feared for them.

'This means that within a few days Guernsey almost certainly will be occupied by German troops. Consequently, starting tomorrow, the Government plans to bring a fleet of boats to the island to evacuate everyone who wishes to leave before the enemy arrives. I must make it quite clear that no one *has* to go. Your parents will tell you whether you are to stay or leave. And they will tell you their own plans.

'The Masters and I have agreed unanimously that we could not continue to provide you with a proper education if the College was operating under a Nazi administration. This means that for the first time since 1563 Elizabeth College will be vacating these buildings and leaving the island, to relocate somewhere in England. For the moment I do not know exactly where that will be.

'The States of Guernsey have arranged that all the schools on the Island will be travelling on the first boats. Consequently the College has to be ready to leave at any time after nine o'clock tomorrow.'

He began to speak more slowly, iterating each word carefully and clearly, and pausing to look at different groups of upturned faces between each sentence. 'Tomorrow morning *all* of you are to come to the College at the normal time for the nine o'clock assembly, even if you are not going with us. There will be a full roll call tomorrow morning.'

He was surprised by the boys' reaction. He had expected them to respond to his news with whispered chatter, and have to be shushed by the prefects, as always happened when he had an unusual announcement to make. But this morning they remained silent, motionless, totally still—even the youngest—as though they sensed the enormity of the situation and the difficulty he was having in conveying the unwanted news to them.

In the front row Le Maitre minor's hair was sticking up in unruly dark tufts, as it always seemed to do no matter how much his mother dabbed at it with his father's Brylcreem. (Sometimes one could even smell it, she used so much!) Nine years old just last week, his grey jersey was creased and dusty, and his cheeks still glowed pink, evidence of his running and scuffling in the courtyard during the break.

Half way down the hall, sitting against the aisle, Keith Beauchamp looked frankly surprised. Last September his parents had travelled from Canterbury with the boy for his arrival as a border at the College. They had sat in the Headmaster's study where the boy's bank-manager father, wearing a dark pinstripe suit and resting a black Trilby hat on his knees, explained that they had chosen Elizabeth College for young Keith '…because Guernsey is such a safe place to be, well away from the route German bombers will take on their way to London and the Midlands.' Now young Keith would be facing a journey to the mainland that could be far more dangerous than anything his parents had faced in Canterbury so far in this strange war.

Standing upright at the back of the hall, with a College First Eleven cricket badge woven onto the breast pocket of his blazer, sixth-former David de Carteret had applied for a commission with the Royal Fusiliers and was likely to be accepted, despite his youth, because of his proficiency as an officer cadet with the O.T.C.—the College's Officer Training Corps. Yet on the surface he seemed a most unlikely candidate, an enigma in fact. Top of his class in literature and divinity, he had an intuitive flair for writing poetry and philosophical treatises far beyond his years. He was a gentle, reflective young man, yet an upright, sharp-looking officer cadet with a commanding presence as a platoon leader. The Headmaster taught divinity to the Sixth Form—as well as to most others—and until this year had felt that de Carteret was clearly cut out for a career in the Ministry.

For himself, he was having difficulty controlling the ache in his throat. He was about to see *his* school uprooted, possibly never to return. But it was even worse for his boys, who were about to be separated from their parents. He sensed that many parents would be unwilling to leave, and if they approved their sons' departure—as he expected most would—there would be no communication between them for as long as the island was occupied.

'After assembly you are to return to your form rooms, where your form Master will give you a piece of paper with information and instructions for your parents.' Their parents were to sign in one of two places, either authorizing the College to transport their son to England and to care for him until the College eventually returned to Guernsey, or signifying that they would be keeping their son in Guernsey.

'When you come to school tomorrow, if you will be leaving with the College you are to bring three things with you:' (He leaned forward to stress the word 'three'.)

'First, your school books, in a satchel that can be carried on your back, over the shoulders like a knapsack. If you have more books than you can carry, your form Master will decide which you are to take.' (Later, the boys chortled that it was typical of

'W.H.G.' to talk about school books *before* mentioning the food and clothing they were to carry. To their ears he had clearly listed everything backwards.)

'Second, a suitcase of clothing, but only as much as you can carry. There will be no luggage service on this trip!' The boys dutifully chuckled at his attempt at humour. 'A list of suggested items will be provided by your form Master.'

'Third, a cloth or string bag with a drawstring containing enough food to last you for 24 hours. If Porky Watkins was going with you, that would be the heaviest bag he would carry!'

Again the boys laughed: Porky Watkins was famous in the illustrated comics for his prodigious appetite.

'Bring nourishing food, such as meat paste sandwiches, fruit, cheese, and raisins. Try not to bring cakes and cream buns…'

The boys groaned.

'…They are not really nutritious and could cause an upset tummy when you are on the boat'

More groans.

'And do I need to remind you to carry your gas masks?'

Still more groans.

9

19th June 1940: Afternoon

We could hear our mother's voice long before Tony and I raced in through the back door. We had cycled home in record time, pedalling our gearless bikes frantically up Les Merriennes rather than dismounting and pushing them up the steep hill as we normally did, both eager to be the first to thrust his instructions into his mother's hands.

'Yes, Anne-Marie, I know its difficult…But Pierre's ten now, isn't he?…No, we'll be sending Ian with the college boys, and he's only nine… I know Pierre's an only child, but…It depends on what you think will be best for him…'

Our mother always talked loudly when she spoke on the telephone. The cone-shaped mouthpiece was hinged to the front of the box at about the level of her forehead. She would pull it down toward her and lift her head up toward it and speak as if she was on the platform at Central Hall addressing cadets taking part in a St John Ambulance first aid course. We suspected—we knew—she was a little deaf, a condition she steadfastly refused to recognize. And we had learned never even to hint at it.

'…What does Tom think you should do?…He's made up his mind to stay?…You have no-one you could live with in England?…Few of us have, Anne-Marie…We'll be assigned to lodgings I expect…No, I really can't advise you what to do. You and Tom will have to decide that…How does Pierre feel about it…?'

We put our notes on the kitchen table and wandered out into the back garden, over to the two walk-in bird cages we had built. Tony's canaries flittered from perch to perch, looking perkily at us with their dark, inquisitive eyes.

'What are you going to do with them?' I asked, inclining my head toward Tony's cage.

'Dunno, yet. What about you?'

'Find someone to look after them, I expect.'

Tony stood on tiptoe with his nose pressed against the wire, watching his canaries build nests for the second year in a row. Last year there had been two eggs, but neither had hatched and after three weeks he had found them lying cracked on the concrete floor. When he had opened one, expecting to find a curled-up baby canary inside, his hands were covered with a greenish slime that had an atrocious smell.

'They'll never lay if you keep pushing your face up to the wire,' I reminded him. 'You'll frighten them.'

Privately, I was envious that Tony's birds were nesting. My budgerigars in the adjoining cage had never shown the slightest interest in using the wooden nesting boxes I had built for them. All they seemed to do was chatter incessantly and kiss beak-to-beak in their strange social way.

Tony stepped back from the wire. 'The Martels will probably stay here, because of their greenhouses. I'll ask them.'

He turned and ran back into the conservatory, returning a moment later carrying a dusty, dome-shaped bird cage in his left hand, his fingers curled through the ring at the top. The cage swayed erratically as he walked, its swing banging against the bars and the seed and water dishes rattling against their glass retainers.

'I could use Robbie's cage,' he called as he approached, holding the cage out in front of him. 'It'll be big enough for four….'

And there he stopped, remembering that little Robbie with his grossly twisted left foot had been mine, as was the cage and the bits and pieces flopping noisily about inside it. When Robbie had been introduced into the large outside cage, his deformity had brought out a vicious streak among the other budgies and they had attacked him. Robbie became one of the few pets our mother allowed in the house.

I shrugged. 'You can have it. I can't put seventeen budgies in there.'

Who could I ask? The Martels would say 'yes,' I knew—they were that kind of people—but Tony was already asking them to take care of his canaries. And really they lived too far away. There were too many budgies to take anywhere, and I didn't have a portable cage, not one that was large enough. And most people didn't like the chattery noise they made, or the mess when they shed their feathers and scattered their seed husks. No, it would have to be someone nearby who was staying on the island; someone who would care enough to come up and feed the budgies. Every day.

To set them free would be tantamount to giving them a death sentence: they would starve without their tropical seeds and the wild birds would attack them, attracted by their bright colours. Eighteen months ago there had been a ferocious autumn gale. A searching south wind had treated the cages' corrugated iron roofs like a ship's sail, billowing them upwards until the cages had been lifted off their concrete bases and flipped onto their backs. In tears, Tony had crept through the open bottom of his canaries' sleeping quarters and had found his four birds terrified but safe, crouched in a corner under the eaves.

But the hardier budgies had gone. Finding a gaping expanse open to the world, they had seized the opportunity to escape or—more likely—had been plucked from their corners by the searching wind. I had written a small advertisement asking people who found stray budgies to return them, and my father had placed it in his newspaper, but we both really knew the birds had not survived the night. The budgies I had now were replacements I had saved up for and bought—sometimes with my parents' help—one or two at a time over the past year and a half.

In my bedroom I pulled up the hinged seat of the old-fashioned two-seat school desk my grandfather had given me on my twelfth birthday. Stepping into the space I had created, I crouched down and reached under the varnished oak writing surface to a narrow shelf at the back of the kneehole. From it I pulled out a wooden pencil box and carried it over to the bed. I pushed on its top with my thumb, watched the lid slid back like a roll-top desk, and lifted out the upper tray of pens and pencils. Below it there were two compartments, one containing pen nibs and an ink eraser, the other an assortment of coins. Holding the palm of one hand over the nib compartment, I flipped the box over so that the coins fell out and scattered silently onto the eiderdown.

There were a shilling, three sixpences, two tiny silver threepenny pieces, seven pennies, a halfpenny, two farthings, and four doubles: three shillings and eightpence without the Guernsey doubles, which at one-eighth of a penny were no longer legal tender. It would have to do.

As I wheeled my bike out through the side gate I could see Tony crouched almost motionless inside the canary's cage, his arms outstretched in front of him with the palms cupped upward. He was creeping very slowly toward a canary clinging to the wire, its head cocked in a questioning attitude. Tony's stealth must have been successful for already one of the canaries was hopping about uncertainly in the small cage at his feet.

'I have just small bags: sixpence-halfpenny each,' the elderly shop assistant explained.

'You don't have any large bags?'

'That's what I said, son.'

'Oh.' Normally I bought five-pound bags of seed from the feed shop in The Bordage, sometimes even ten pounds when I had enough pocket money. But it was too far to cycle into St Peter Port now, so I had cycled the half mile to Le Riche's grocery shop near the Old Mill. 'How much do they weigh?'

The shop assistant disappeared among the shelves behind the counter and returned with a brown-paper bag, which he dropped onto one platform of a pair of scales. He slipped weights onto the other platform until the two sides hovered equal-height above the counter top. 'Sixteen ounces,' he announced. 'One pound exactly.'

'Can I have six then, please?' I had already calculated that six would cost three shillings and threepence, which would leave me fivepence. It was much more expensive than buying from the feed store, where a five-pound bag cost only one shilling and ninepence.

The shop assistant returned with four more bags, which he lined up on the counter. 'That's all I have,' he said laconically. 'Two and eightpence-halfpenny.'

I counted out the coins. 'Could you put them in a larger bag, please? I've got to carry them on my bike.'

I cycled home the long way round, along Rue Poudreuse to the top of Les Merrienes, rather than dive down the steep hill past St Martin's church with the bags of seed held in one hand. As I rounded the corner at the top of La Bellieuse I could see my father's Vauxhall standing beside the hedge in front of Wendy Cotte.

In the back garden he was digging a hole with a spade, a cardboard box standing beside him. He had taken off his jacket and pulled on rubber boots, but he still wore his waistcoat and tie.

I thought one of the animals must have died and my father was going to bury it. I walked across, pulled back the cardboard lid, and saw to my surprise that it contained about twenty copies of *Norman Ten Hundred*, the book my father had written about the Guernsey Light Infantry in the 1914-1918 war.

'You're burying your books?' I was incredulous.

'It's better to.'

'But why, Dad?'

'I don't want to leave any evidence for the Germans, when they come. I name people in it who fought against them in France; lots of people who are still living on the island, and they may stay here. I could be putting them in danger, if the Germans feel like being vindictive.'

'But your books!'

'I know.'

'You'll keep one?'

My father shook his head. 'No. That part of my life's over.' Seeing my dismay, he added: 'You'll understand one day.'

I reached into the box and lifted out one of the slim khaki-coloured volumes. Its cover announced in large, dark, navy-blue letters:

Norman
Ten
Hundred
by
A Stanley Blicq

I opened the cover and read:

> **A Battalion of the Oldest and Smallest Democracy in the World**
>
> Guernsey—named Sarnia by the Romans—one of the Channel Isles from out the sun swathed romance of whose shores rallied a fierce band of Norman warriors to the aid of their Duke , William of Normandy, afterwards the Conqueror, at Hastings, 1066. In reward for their valour William granted the Isles the independence they maintain to this day. From Guernsey something approaching 7,000 men have gone out into the Great Undertaking.
>
> The Norman Ten Hundred is the 1st Royal Guernsey Light Infantry offered by the States of Guernsey for active participation in the Great War (1914-1918).

I realized then I had never read my father's book. I felt I should have, but I had never seen a copy on the living room bookshelves. When I was about twelve I had asked him about it; if I could read it. He had hesitated momentarily, and then said: 'Not now. When you are older, perhaps. There's time enough.'

I leafed through the brown-edged pages until the letters 's-i-iz-z…kr-rupp!' caught my eye. I read more:

The inscrutable ways of chance—Destiny, call it what you will—brought about the greatest catastrophe that so far obtained in the Guernsey ranks. Major Davey moved his party over an area at about 11 in the morning of a warm, sunny Sunday—coming in for a spell of shelling extraordinary in intensity. A labour unit retired because of the exigencies of the precarious situation. Inflexible, the Normans carried on, then *s-i-iz-z…kr-rupp!*

The leading platoon caught it in their very midst, a ghastly heap of mangled flesh and shattered limbs were scattered to right and left. Two unhappy lads were blown to unrecognisable fragments. No words can convey the heart-rending cries of those whose bodies cringe and writhe from the hell-hot agony of searing shrapnel. There is an unmistakable appeal for pity that stirs the depth of feeling until a wild frenzy to right matters sends Berserk passion to the brain. Oh, you German gunners in your serene safety, if ever my chance comes…!

Thus the first of the Ten Hundred went over the Great Divide.

An order to retire was quietly obeyed….

Following a brief rest the 29th Division trained from Poperinghe southwards. The same weary cooping in cattle-trucks, same monotonous crawl. And yet during a halt at Hazebrucke arose one of those moments that live long in memory, when patriotism rises high in the breast. The station was crowded with soldiers and civilians as the Guernseys' train drew up in the cool, dusky evening light. Someone played a cornet: 'The long, long trail.' From end to end of the train the Ten Hundred caught it up and sang low in their soft southern accent. A hush fell on the chattering onlookers, they turned and stared. The harmony enveloped them, stirred them …and we, ah, how the blood stirs even now. But the memory saddens—for the voices of many are for ever still. *

'Put it back in the box,' my father said. He said it gently, as if he had not wanted to intrude.

As I closed the cover I saw a dedication page at the front and paused to read it:

- A Stanley Blicq, *Norman Ten Hundred*, Guernsey Evening Press, 1920.

This modest work is dedicated to
Mrs. P. EREAUX
in appreciation of her genial personality, strong moral courage and unhesitating adherence to duty as she conceived it.

Patricia Ereaux was my father's grandmother, the woman who had brought my father up.

And also to:
GEORGE W. CLARKE, ESQ.,
In memory of those Great Days when we marched the Long Trail together; shared the same sorrows, the same mirth; -- and now the same memories, far away, indistinct; laughter merged with the tears.

Now I was puzzled. When Tony and I were younger, my father had told us bedtime stories about the adventures he and Knobby Clarke had in France. Funny stories. Nothing like this. It was as if he was a different person. It didn't even sound like him, not the way he talked.

Reluctantly, I laid the book on top of the pile.

The hole was now about 20 inches across and two feet deep, with a mound of rich loam standing beside it. My father thrust the end of the spade upright into the mound and lifted the box into the hole. It stuck about one-third of the way down. He lifted it out, grabbed the spade, and shaved earth from the sides.

'You can do something for me, if you want,' he grunted between strokes.

'What?'

'Find a way to get the chickens into Mr Frome's field.' Seeing the surprised look on my face, he added: 'He's going to look after them for us, but he doesn't want to come up here, or bother with the cages. Says he'll let them roam free, to hunt and peck, like his do.'

It was a little over a year ago—before the war started—that our father suddenly began importing day old chicks from a hatchery in England. Every two weeks he would waken me at 5:30 and we would drive sleepily down through the town and out onto the White Rock, the pier. When the mailboat from Southampton arrived we would stand at the foot of the gangplank waiting for a docker to carry a large, flat cardboard box down to us, which we would carry carefully to the car and lower gently onto the back seat. The box was warm to the touch and from it came little scratching sounds and tiny cheeps.

On the floor of an empty dog kennel my father had placed a paraffin lamp within a protective metal shield and had lit it before we left home. By the time we returned the lamp had warmed the kennel, and when the chicks were let out of the box they crowded around it seeking the warmth of their absent mother.

Not all the chicks arrived alive. Usually the mortality rate was low, no more than five or six in a box of one hundred, although on one stormy morning the boat had been late and the box had been strangely quiet when we carried it to the car. We had driven home rapidly to find that only seven of the chicks had survived the journey, and even they were barely alive.

My father had been upset, but not nearly as upset as my mother, whose silence spoke eloquently of her disapproval. First it had been the spaniels, the building of the kennels at the expense of garden space, and then the noisy barking, and above all the cost. True, the dogs were pedigreed bitches and had won blue ribands every year at the dog show, but the pups they had borne still didn't bring in the large sums he had predicted. And now it was this hair-brained scheme to keep chickens—hundreds of them!—taking up more garden space and more than likely creating a smell. They might as well live on a farm!

'It won't be like that at all,' he had tried to explain during a dinner, when the electricity crackled from one end of the table to the other and the three boys ate in silence and finished their meals as quickly as possible so they could be excused from the table. 'The hens will be up off the ground. In batteries they call it. It's a new method. You won't have them underfoot and they'll take up only a little bit of space.'

She sniffed a barely audible 'Humph.'

'And there won't be a smell, because the droppings can be shovelled up every day: they'll be all in one place.'

There was no response.

'If there's a war and there's rationing, there'll be a demand for food like this….'

On the evening of the thirteenth day he would transfer the two-week-old chicks to a larger cage, still in a shed but now unheated, and the following day he and I would fetch a new batch of day-olds and introduce them to their proxy mother hen. Meanwhile he had started building a long frame-like structure on the tennis-size lawn that stretched across the bottom of the garden. He drove two rows of stakes into the lawn, about thirty inches apart and four feet high, and connected them along the top and half way up the sides with horizontal strips of two-inch square lumber. Around the upper part of the structure he wrapped chicken wire, forming a long tube two feet off the ground, nailed and tar-papered a roof over the top, and hung feed and water trays on either side. Now the pens were filled with hens in various stages of growth, and the first batch had been sent to market. Even my mother had been surprised at the good price they fetched.

I let out a dozen hens at a time. I tried herding them toward the gap in the earth bank that separated the bottom of our garden from Mr Frome's upper field, but the hens were an unruly lot. It was as if they resented being released from the security of their cages and either huddled in little groups, unsure what to do, or flapped clumsily into the air only to flutter lamely into the bushes on top of the bank.

An hour later I shooed the last birds through the gap and paused for a moment, a little breathless, my feet straddling the top of the bank. Below me, the white and brown hens were bobbing their way down the field in a widening band as they hunted and pecked toward the pigsty at the foot of the slope.

I turned and looked back toward our bungalow. My father had transplanted clumps of rhubarb onto the space where he had been digging, and had tamped the earth down with the back of a spade. Where the rhubarb had been he had spread the earth loosely round, as if he had been digging there, presumably to fool anyone who might search.

In the kitchen my mother was slicing a Hovis loaf for our tea. She buttered the bread farmhouse style, spreading the butter on the cut end of the loaf before slicing off each piece.

The *Guernsey Evening Press* was lying folded on the kitchen table, where my father had dropped it when he came in. I picked it up and carried it into my bedroom. Across the top of the front page a headline broadcast in bold letters:

EVACUATION OF CHILDREN

And below it there were two subheads:

PARENTS MUST REPORT THIS EVENING

Clothing and Ration Necessities

Guernsey, Wednesday 19 June 1940: Arrangements are being made for the evacuation of (1) children of school age and (2) children under school age to reception areas in the United Kingdom under Government arrangement.

The evacuation is expected to take place to-morrow, the 20th June, 1940.

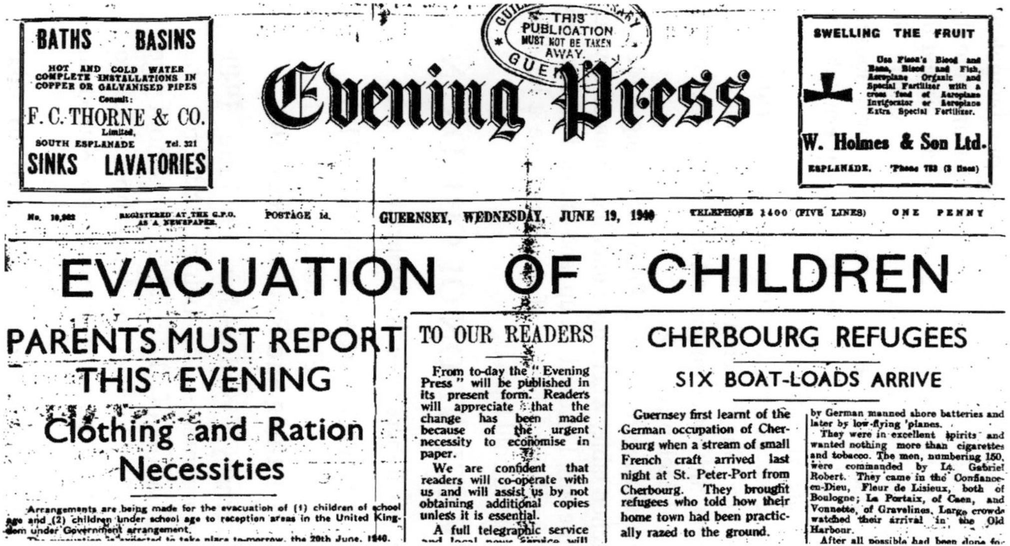

BATHS BASINS

HOT AND COLD WATER COMPLETE INSTALLATIONS IN COPPER OR GALVANISED PIPES

Consult:

F. C. THORNE & CO.
Limited,
SOUTH ESPLANADE Tel. 321

SINKS LAVATORIES

THIS PUBLICATION MUST NOT BE TAKEN AWAY.

Evening Press

SWELLING THE FRUIT

Use Fison's Blood and Bone, Blood and Fish, Aeroplane Organic and Special Fertilizer with a cross feed of Aeroplane Invigorator or Aeroplane Extra Special Fertilizer.

W. Holmes & Son Ltd.

ESPLANADE. Phone 753 (3 lines)

No. 10,962 REGISTERED AT THE G.P.O. AS A NEWSPAPER. POSTAGE 1d. GUERNSEY, WEDNESDAY, JUNE 19, 1940 TELEPHONE 1400 (FIVE LINES) ONE PENNY

EVACUATION OF CHILDREN

PARENTS MUST REPORT THIS EVENING

Clothing and Ration Necessities

Arrangements are being made for the evacuation of (1) children of school age and (2) children under school age to reception areas in the United Kingdom under Government arrangement.

The evacuation is expected to take place to-morrow, the 20th June, 1940.

TO OUR READERS

From to-day the "Evening Press" will be published in its present form. Readers will appreciate that the change has been made because of the urgent necessity to economise in paper.

We are confident that readers will co-operate with us and will assist us by not obtaining additional copies unless it is essential.

A full telegraphic service and local news service will

CHERBOURG REFUGEES

SIX BOAT-LOADS ARRIVE

Guernsey first learnt of the German occupation of Cherbourg when a stream of small French craft arrived last night at St. Peter-Port from Cherbourg. They brought refugees who told how their home town had been practically razed to the ground

by German manned shore batteries and later by low-flying 'planes.

They were in excellent spirits and wanted nothing more than cigarettes and tobacco. The men, numbering 150, were commanded by Lt. Gabriel Robert. They came in the Confiance-en-Dieu, Fleur de Lisieux, both of Boulogne; La Portaix, of Caen, and Vonnette, of Gravelines. Large crowds watched their arrival in the Old Harbour.

After all possible had been done for

The Guernsey Evening Press announces the imminent evacuation from the island. The evacuation started the following day.

The mothers of children under school age will be allowed to accompany their children.

Parents of schoolchildren are to attend at the school attended by their children at 7 p.m. to-day to notify their willingness or otherwise for the evacuation of their children.

IF PARENTS DESIRE IT

Parents of children under school age who desire their children evacuated must give the name and address of such children to the Rector or Vicar of their Parish by 8 p.m. to-day. The Rectors will prepare lists accordingly and will transmit them by 10 p.m. to the Bailiff's Office.

Other persons (other than men of military age) desirous of being evacuated must register their names and addresses with the Constables of their parish at the parish Douzaine Room as soon as possible and at latest by 8 p.m. to-day.

All men of military age, i.e., from 20 to 33 years, who desire to be evacuated must register their names and addresses with the Constables of their Parish at the Parish Douzaine Room by 9 p.m.

THEY ARE VERY STRONGLY URGED TO DO SO.

ARTICLES TO TAKE

Children should take with them on evacuation the following articles:

Gas masks.

Two ration books (current and new one).

Besides the clothes which the child will be wearing, which should include an overcoat or mackintosh, a complete change of clothing should be carried. The following is suggested:-

GIRLS	BOYS
One vest or combination	One vest
One pair of knickers	One shirt with collar
One bodice	One pair of pants
One petticoat	One pullover or jersey
Two pairs of stockings	One pair of knickers
Handkerchieves	Handkerchieves
Slip and blouse	Two pairs of socks or Stockings
Cardigan	

Additional for all:- Night attire, comb, towel, soap, face-cloth, toothbrush, and, if possible, boots and shoes and plimsolls. Blankets must not be taken.

THE RATIONS

Rations for the journey: Sandwiches (egg or cheese); Packets of nuts and Seedless raisins; Dry biscuits (with little packets of cheese); Barley sugar (rather than Chocolate); Apple; Orange.

That's the same as the list we were given at school, I thought. *The one I put on the kitchen table.*

Parents of children to be evacuated must attend at the school attended by their children at 9 a.m. to-morrow, the 20th June, to receive instructions as to the final arrangements to be complied with.

Parents of children under school age will attend at the Parish School of the parish in which they reside at 10 a.m. to-morrow, the 20th June, to receive similar instructions.

It will not be possible, on account of the danger of air raids, to permit masses of people to congregate at the harbour and accordingly parents must say au-revoir to their children at their homes or at the Schools. The public will not be permitted to approach the harbour.

Transport to the harbour will be provided as necessary.

On registration for the evacuation of children or adults, it must be stated whether or not financial provision can be made for the maintenance of the evacuee in the United Kingdom and whether or not the evacuee can go to a relative or friend there and the name and address of that relative or friend must be given.

VICTOR G. CAREY,
Bailiff of Guernsey *

For the first time I sensed the enormity of what was about to happen. The early morning news had been fragmented, disconnected. Even Dr Milne's announcement in the College Hall had seemed more like arrangements to be made for a College outing, rather like an O.T.C. exercise, than a real-life set of marching orders.

But reading it like this, in the privacy of my room, introduced a disturbing element of reality. We really were going to have to leave everything we owned, other than what we could personally carry. My treasured HO gauge Hornby train set; the gold Coronation coach with eight horses and mounted soldiers my grandparents had given me in 1937 on the succession of George VI to the throne; my stamp collection; my budgerigars….

At this stage I could think only of my personal losses. That I was about to leave a treasured lifestyle which I could not replicate elsewhere was beyond my imagination. In fact I had no way of knowing what 'elsewhere' would be like: I had never travelled outside the islands. The farthest I had been was a one-week trip to Alderney.

* *Guernsey Evening Press,* Guernsey, C.I., 19 June 1940.

How my parents must be feeling hadn't yet entered into my thoughts. I knew they would have to tell the authorities almost immediately they were willing to send their sons away, and then in a day or so pack up what they could carry and leave everything else they owned (providing there would be enough time for them to get away before the Germans landed). But these seemed like practical decisions they would have to make; steps they would have to take.

Yet, underneath, nagging at me as I went about the practical things that had to be done, I sensed the agony that parents all over the Channel Islands must be facing; the two-pronged dilemma they had to address, and answer within three or four hours. Should they keep their children at home and let them live under the privations and uncertainties and domination of an occupying army? Or should they send their children with their school across the English Channel on what initially would be a dangerous journey, with enemy E-boats, U-boats and fighter-bombers on the watch-out for potential targets?

And what would they be sending them to? To be billeted with strangers? To stay with their school, somewhere "up north"? To be sent as boarders to another school? And how long would it before they would see their children again? If this war was going to be anything like the last, that could be another three years!

At the same time, parents had to be thinking what *they* should do? Should they sacrifice all they own and escape to the mainland? Or should they remain and live under German rule for… for how long?

Yet the full impact of what parents must be feeling would not really occur to me until many years later, after I had grown into adulthood and had a family and possessions of my own.

I folded the newspaper carefully and carried it back into the kitchen, placing it on the same place on the table.

'I hope you've not been touching the clothes I've laid out on your bed,' my mother cautioned, pointing a buttery knife toward me. 'I don't want you moving anything until I've checked them against my list.'

Nothing has changed! I thought.

Aloud I asked: 'Did you put in my air raid helmet?'

'Good gracious, no! It's much too heavy.'

'I could wear it.'

'You'll be expected to wear your college cap, like everyone else.'

I went into the bathroom to wash for tea, leaving the door open into the passage.

'Will you be going into the office tomorrow?' That was my mother's voice.

'Yes. For a while.'

'What's the point? You've already told Peake you're going.'

'I know. But I'd rather hand over properly.'

'Who's going to be news editor?'

'Billy Vaudin. He knows already.'

'He's staying?'

'So he says.'

'Then why bother to go in?'

'I want to write my last editorial. Until we come back.'

I was surprised at the authority in my father's voice. I was equally surprised that my mother should accept his decision almost without demur, also a rare occurrence. At the same time I felt vaguely troubled that they should be discussing such a momentous event so unemotionally. I realized that the speed at which events had been thrust upon them had given little time for reflection, but did our parents really have to treat their imminent separation from their children so matter-of-factly?

True, I felt safer, more protected from my feelings this way. I didn't have time to think about the consequences, or the terrible decisions every parent on the island must be facing, *right now.*

10

19th June 1940: Evening

'The Martels will be only too happy to look after the canaries for me,' Tony announced, parroting Mrs Martel's exact words.

'Oh? How are they?' our mother enquired, referring to the Martels although she hardly knew them. She handed a teacup to Tony, to pass to his father at the far end of the long dining table.

The Martels were growers, which meant they grew tomatoes and flowers in long, glass greenhouses that captured the sun and brought their crop in early, to gain a good export price. Their son David was accepted as a friend for Tony because the two boys had attended the Intermediate School together. Then after two years Tony was moved to Elizabeth College and, although our parents did not actually discourage his friendship with David, they did covertly encourage him to be friendly with Paul Ozanne, the son of a solicitor, who was in the same Form at the College.

'They're fine,' Tony replied, reaching for the raspberry jam and again echoing Mrs Martel's words. 'Mrs Martel says they can't leave, what with the tomatoes and flowers being ready. But David's going.'

'No jam!' our mother cautioned, pointing a finger at the plate in front of Tony. 'That's Guernsey butter on that bread. Take the bread with New Zealand butter, if you want jam on it.'

Guernsey butter, made only from rich, creamy milk from Guernsey cows, was a natural golden colour and considered much too tasty (and expensive) to have its unique flavour disguised by a savoury or sweet covering.

If casual onlookers were to peep into the Wendy Cotte windows right now, I thought, *they would think they were watching an average middle-class family eating a normal tea of buttered bread, scones, salmon-paste and cucumber sandwiches, watercress, and jam-filled cake. Even if they heard the conversation, they would assume they were listening to a mother, father, and their three sons engaged in everyday tea-time conversation. They would have to listen very closely to catch the real meaning behind the words. How could we be so damned dispassionate?*

'What do you want me to put in your sandwiches?' our mother asked, as if she was planning a picnic at Portelet. 'I'll make them tonight.'

'Crab paste!' nine-year old Ian mumbled, a cucumber sandwich clutched between the fingers of his two hands.

'*One* hand, Ian, if you please. Preferably your left, for sandwiches and bread and butter. And don't speak with your mouth full.'

Ian dropped his right hand into his lap and swallowed obediently. 'Crab paste, please.'

'Ummm…I'm not sure how well crab-paste will travel. Marmite would be better.'

'All right. Marmite.'

It was a rare child who did not like the yeast and vegetable-based compound known as Marmite, which was reputed to be full of vitamin B2 and was so strong that it had to be applied thinly to bread and sparingly in soups and broths. Our father even liked stirring it into hot milk, as a cold-weather drink when he came in from working among the chickens or in the dog run. We children had tried it but wrinkled our noses and couldn't agree it was pleasant. Ovaltine was much better.

'With your sandwiches,' our mother continued, 'you'll each have a slice of cheese, two apples, and a small bag of raisins, for energy.'

Our father placed the palms of his hands flat on the tablecloth and leaned toward us three boys, the two younger ones sitting beside each other on one long side of the large dining table and the eldest sitting alone on the other, under the window. He cleared his throat with a small cough: 'I want you to do something for me,' he said, in a confidential but deliberate manner. 'I don't want you to go swapping your food for the stuff other boys bring, no matter how attractive it may look. Just remember your mother will have spent a lot of time preparing what you're taking with you, and you'll know it'll all be fresh, something you can't be sure of if you take food from anyone else. You won't know how long it has been sitting around in other people's larders, and it could easily have gone off. Food like that can make you pretty ill, and very quickly.'

Prudent, cautious, and careful, I thought. Those would be the adjectives I'd use if I had to describe my father in an essay. *What a strange family we are: here we are talking about leaving Guernsey for Lord knows how long, but we all act as though we are just going on a day trip. Nobody has even discussed whether we should leave, or what the implications are of staying or leaving. When the Headmaster told us what was to happen, I thought we'd all go home and talk it over with our parents. At least that's what the other boys in the Fourth Form thought they'd be doing.*

Do we always have to do the 'right thing,' automatically? I know Mummy's on top form in a crisis; that's why she always just takes over, and people stand back and let her do it. I suppose that's why she's a bigwig in the St John Ambulance Brigade, too, like Grandpa was. It's no wonder, really, what with him and two of her brothers being officers in the army.

Had our parents really ***talked*** *to each other about whether the family should stay or leave? And whether my brothers and I should go even if they choose to stay? Shouldn't we be discussing it now, as a family, while we're here all together around the dining table? That*, I imagined, *is what would be happening in other people's homes.*

I briefly considered bringing up the subject, and as quickly decided not to. After all, if my parents preferred to maintain a calm, matter-of-fact approach to what was really a critical event, then perhaps I should too. But I couldn't help wondering what their real objective was: to instil confidence and a sense of normalcy in their children—particularly the younger two—or, by simply not addressing the problem, to insulate themselves from their true feelings? That way they would be better able to contain their emotions, to maintain their accustomed traditional British phlegm.

'You and Tony can take your bikes to school in the morning, as you usually do,' our father said. 'I'll take your suitcases and books with me in the car, when I drive Ian to school. You can leave a little early, then meet me at the College gate.'

*

While my brothers helped our mother clear the table and dry the dishes, my father stepped down into the conservatory and stood beside me. I was pouring the five bags of seed I had purchased into a tall biscuit tin.

'I want you to help me put the dogs in the car.'

'The dogs?' The dogs were never allowed in the car.

'They can't stay here. No-one will feed them.'

'Where will you take them?'

'The G.S.P.C.A. They'll look after them.' He must have seen the doubt in my eyes, for he added (I suspected with more confidence than he felt): 'I telephoned. It's all arranged.'

When we entered the kennel with collars and leads in our hands, the five female dogs milled around our feet, wagging their stump tails and twisting their rumps in the strange, affectionate way that spaniels have. Barney—the sole male dog—paced impatiently back and forth outside the length of fence that kept him away from the five females. He had already sensed that a change in routine signalled something out of the ordinary was about to happen.

Wendy, the compliant seven-year-old, mother of Judy and Sally, stood patiently beside me as I slipped the leather collar around her neck and tightened it until it was a little short of snug. Wendy was my favourite. From a 'show' point of view she was not the best of the six golden spaniels my father owned, but she had won her share of honours at the island's annual two-day dog show and had given birth to more than a handful of potential champions. She had been sent to England for a week when she was three years old, where she was teamed with best-of-show winner 'Walter of Somerset,' and subsequently had produced a litter of seven, six of whom had survived and five had been sold for respectable sums. My father decided to keep the best of the litter and named her Judy. Later he had imported Barney, a male champion from the mainland, who had sired Sally with Wendy, and Tilly and Megs with Judy. Barney had the honour of running free and sleeping in a tea chest laid on its side in the conservatory, although he was never allowed in the house.

The four other females wriggled and cavorted, their communal excitement transmitted from one to the other and making useless my father's exhorted commands of 'Down!' and 'Sit!'

Their excitement continued in the small Vauxhall, where they jumped from the back seat down to the floor and then back up again, and tried to stick their heads between the front seats hoping for a hand to lick or that my father would pat them.

'They're not accustomed to the freedom,' my father explained. 'Or the car.'

'It's all a big adventure for them,' I agreed from the left-hand seat, and then laughed as one of the dogs poked me in the shoulder with her chin and nuzzled my left ear. I turned and saw it was Wendy, who had placed her rear feet on the back seat and supported her front paws on the back of my seat. I leant back and scratched her floppy ears.

'Wendy's always had a soft spot for you,' my father said.

It was true. As the kennel population increased, entering the dogs in the different classes in the dog show became more difficult for one person to handle alone. At first my mother had helped, but in recent years my father had arranged for me to be absent from school for the two days, so I could show one of the dogs when two were entered in simultaneous or consecutive events. My father had suggested I should work with Wendy, because she would be the easiest to handle and conceivably might gain a second or third place.

But Wendy seemed to understand I was green and displayed an unexpected ring sense when I nervously led her into the ring for the first time. As soon as the nine dogs and their owners were spaced to the judge's satisfaction, I squatted beside Wendy and slid the back of my left hand gently under her neck, ready to exert a slight upward pressure to elevate her head. I was about to slip the palm of my right hand under her belly to encourage her to stand properly, when I saw she had already adopted the stance favoured by judges. Her head was held high, her body leaned slightly forward, her back legs were spread about nine inches apart, and her short tail was straight and horizontal to the ground. She looked every inch a champion.

I scratched her gently under the chin and whispered into her ear: 'Good girl, Wendy; well done.' Then I stood up and allowed the lead to fall in a long, loose loop from my hand to her collar.

Across the ring my father was patiently coaxing Megs, who had been entered in competition judging for the first time but really was too young and frisky and constantly turned around to sniff at the spaniels on either side.

The judge approached, nodded to me, and bent down beside Wendy, stroking the top of her head. 'Good lass,' he said in a noticeable Scots accent, and looked up at me: 'What do you call her?'

'Wendy, sir.'

With the palm of his hand the judge felt the curved dome of her head, and then gripped the front of each thigh, first the forelegs and then the rear. 'I'll wager that's your daughter over yon,' he murmured to her, consulting his program and tilting his head in Meg's direction. 'Or your granddaughter. Eh, lass?'

The dog barely moved, apart from a slight twitch of her tail to acknowledge that she had heard him.

The judge stood up. 'Walk her over there, lad,' he said, pointing diagonally across the ring, 'and then run back.'

'Come, Wendy,' I said, and she obediently trotted beside me, her head held high and the lead still hanging loosely from my hand. On reaching the opposite side of the ring (which really was square with two rows of seats around its four sides), I turned on my heel, allowed her to turn around me, and then broke into a gentle run. Wendy changed her gait to a lope but remained beside me, looking straight ahead. She made no attempt to frisk about as some dogs did, thinking it was an invitation to play when their owners broke into a run.

'Thank you,' the judge said as he turned to the next spaniel. 'You handle her well.'

From the far side of the ring I could sense my father's approval, but dared not look up for fear I might grin foolishly or, worse, break into a blush. Instead I bent down and stroked Wendy's head and patted her on the rump. 'Oh, well done, Wendy. You are a good girl.' Again her tail twitched slightly, but this time she turned her head toward me and gave my hand a single lick.

So a bond was formed and a tradition was set. From that day on, Wendy was to be my show dog. And together we won ribbons and medals until her age and repeated motherhood began to take their toll and give her a matron's figure.

'Did you remember to bring the food?' I asked, breaking a protracted silence.

'Food?'

'Dog food.'

'They – er – they said they didn't need it. They've got lots.'

'Oh.' I thought about this for a while. I wasn't quite sure whether my father was allowing his innate kindness—his unwillingness to hurt—to colour his reply, to influence his natural honesty. We were in the Câtel now, travelling down a narrow, high-hedged lane I did not recognize. Long grasses brushed the side of the car.

'This is Les Truchots.'

'Oh!' I replied. Then I blurted out: 'What will they do with the dogs?'

'Find new homes for them, I expect.' My father kept looking straight ahead—keeping an eye on the road, he called it—not pausing even momentarily to glance toward me.

'But…if everyone's leaving…?' I left the question unfinished.

'Not everyone will leave.'

'Oh.' Yet I could not really comprehend why anyone should want to stay. I had been caught up in the sheer exhilaration of the adventure that was happening. Only eight hours had elapsed since the Headmaster's momentous announcement, and I had not had time to reflect on the almost unthinkable decisions that had been thrust overnight on practically every adult on the island.

'People who stay here will want protection,' my father continued, feeling perhaps he should elaborate, 'particularly if the island is to be occupied by the enemy. I expect a lot of people who don't have a dog now will be looking for one. As a guard dog.'

'Then the dogs won't be able to stay together?'

'Our dogs? No, it's unlikely.' We were descending and approaching a sharp right-hand bend. 'Ah, This is it: Les Fiers Moutons.'

He slowed the car to a crawl and pulled as far to the left as he could, so my side of the car brushed against the grasses and nettles growing out of the earth hedge. At the bend he swung the Vauxhall in a tight 180-degree turn into a gravelled gateway with the letters G.S.P.C.A. printed on a board clamped onto an open wrought-iron gate.

The Guernsey Society for the Prevention of Cruelty to Animals proved to be a private bungalow with large wire pens set well back in what had once been the back garden. A chorus of barks and yelps erupted as the car's wheels crunched on the gravel. A middle-aged man emerged from the side of the house, collarless in a striped shirt and wearing a dark unbuttoned waistcoat over it.

The dogs tumbled out of the car, creating a tangle of leather dog leads. The man leant a hand forward, ready to grasp some of the leads.

'*No!*'

My father's voice was unexpectedly sharp. 'We'll manage, thanks.'

The man stepped back and waited while father and son sorted out the dogs until we each held three leads. We led the dogs around the side of the house to a row of vertically barred gates, each opening into a long, narrow dog run. Some 15 or 20 dogs ran barking to the gates, those in front jumping up and placing their forefeet on a crossbar about 24 inches above the ground.

'Bitches in here. Males over there.' The man pointed to a second set of gates further to our left, with more dogs in them.

'Here, I'll hold Barney,' my father said, and he looped the male dog's lead through the wire and formed a loose knot. 'Now, let's get this lot inside.'

I had wondered how they were going to open the gates without some of the dogs escaping, but now saw that the man was pulling on a rope that fed over a pulley high on the gate post. A sliding trap door set within the gate inched slowly upward. We pushed the five dogs through, one after the other, snapping their leads undone as they went.

'The kennels were made for just one or two dogs,' the man explained. 'I've had to fill them up, so many people have been bringing their dogs in.'

My father nodded and handed the five empty leads dangling from his hand.

'I'll take Barney over there,' he said to me. 'You can say good-night to Wendy.'

He unknotted Barney's lead and walked to the other gate, the dog trotting beside him with the familiar, proud, elegant yet awkward gait we had all come to know. Barney had been my father's favourite from the day he arrived from England aboard the St Patrick, his black nose pushed against the wire mesh at one end of the shipping chest.

I squatted in front of the bitches' cage and wrapped my fingers around the crossbar above my head. 'Wendy!' I called.

The dogs were silent now, milling around and cautiously sniffing the newcomers.

'Wendy!' I called again, and saw her lift her head and turn in my direction. 'Here, girl!' She padded toward me, her tail twisting back and forth.

'Now you be a good girl, Wen.' I said, wondering what one should say at such a moment. 'You're the oldest so just keep an eye on the others. Make sure they're all right.' She licked the fingers of my left hand, until Megs frisked over and nuzzled her away. 'Hello, Megs,' I continued, 'and you look after your grandma. Do you hear me?'

The other dogs came crowding toward the wire, pushing and shoving as each demanded her share of attention. Wendy was pushed aside by the pack.

I stood up. 'G'night, Wen,' I called. ''Night, Megs.'

There was a painted sign beside the gate and I wandered over to read it:

IN 1939 THE G.S.P.C.A. –

	Dogs	***Cats***
Provided homes for strays and unwanted pets:	111	263
Provided care and treatment for:	112	260
Painlessly destroyed for owners:	272	321

The Guernsey Society for the Prevention of Cruelty to Animals depends entirely on bequests and contributions. It is not States supported.

As I turned away from the sign I caught a momentary glimpse of my father surreptitiously handing the man several pound notes, and the man equally surreptitiously tucking them into a waistcoat pocket.

We drove home in silence, the sun now low behind us. Although I partly sensed my father's pain, it would be nearly thirty years before I fully understood the depth of his grief. Then I would be an adult of about the same age with two sons of my own, and would be forced to dispose of Blackie, a treasured black spaniel. And a decade later, when my daughter was 15 as I was now, together we would have to ask the vet to 'painlessly destroy' Rogue, a devoted, gentle, majestic Alsation who suffered from gradually worsening epileptic fits.

My father cleared his throat with a double subdued cough that I had long recognized portended an announcement; something that he found difficult to articulate and probably had been turning over in his mind for several minutes.

'I want you to do something for me,' he started.

I wondered whether I was expected to respond, but decided just to turn my head toward him and wait.

'You and your brothers will be on your own for a while, and that puts quite a responsibility on you.' Again he cleared his throat; again with a double cough. 'Your mother and I are, well, we are rather depending on you, as the eldest, to keep an eye out for your brothers, particularly Ian. You'll be taking our places, really, and it's important for them to know you're there, if they need someone to talk to. I don't mean you've got to be with them every minute, but just look in on them from time to time. Do you know what I mean?'

For a moment he took his eyes away from the road and glanced toward me.

'Yes, I think so,' I answered. I looked briefly toward him, then turned away.

'Tony and Ian have never been away from home before—not on their own, as you have—and sometimes they may need a little reassurance.'

He drew the car to a halt at a yellow line—we were at Bailiff's Cross now—and looked to left and right. Then he inched the car into the intersection.

I wondered what kind of response he expected. I had reached the age when I tended to listen to my parents' homilies with carefully concealed impatience. Yet this was different. My father was a deeply feeling but reticent man, and was clearly struggling to find the right words. It was strange that he could readily write a stirring editorial for his newspaper, but could not easily talk to his eldest son about a sensitive or personal matter.

'We won't be far behind you. We won't be far away.'

'Do you know when you'll be leaving?'

'No, not exactly.' Then, choosing his words carefully, he added: 'Your mother and I will be on one of the first boats, after the school children. I can promise you that.'

I thought for a moment. 'Do you have any idea where we'll be, in England?'

'No.' He shook his head emphatically. 'No idea. I expect you'll be told when you disembark, just as we will.' He smiled thinly. 'It's a safe bet you won't be anywhere in the southeast. The west country, more likely.'

11

20th June 1940: Afternoon

By three o'clock the following afternoon every Master was wishing one of the prefects would knock on his classroom door to announce the college was on its way. Even though assembly had taken longer than usual, and the Masters had supervised the selection and packing—and repacking—of the books that each boy would carry, by 11 a.m. their pupils were sitting expectantly at their desks, each with a suitcase, satchel of books, gasmask, and lunch bag piled beside him. The Masters wondered what to do to keep the boys occupied—it was out of the question to try teaching anything—and in the ensuing four hours they had drawn puzzles, games and contests on the blackboard, and allowed the boys outside twice for extended play sessions which they called 'free exercise.'

At 3:30 the headmaster sent prefects around with a note saying that nothing would happen before 8 p.m., and suggested the Masters allow older boys who lived within twenty minutes walking distance go home for a while.

Mr Waite announced with some relief that Town House boys who lived in St Peter Port could leave, and about one-third of the boys in the Fourth Form scrambled out of the room followed by his bellowed admonishment: 'And you're to be back, sitting at your desks, by a quarter to seven. At the very latest!'

I was in Town House, but I didn't live in St Peter Port so the release didn't apply to me. But I was bored and I wanted to see what was happening at home. So I waited until the noise of hurrying shoes had subsided down the flagstone passage, then rose from my desk and stepped up onto the platform at the front of the room.

'I've got my bike here, sir,' I half-whispered, 'and I live in St Martins and I'm in Town House. Is it all right if I go too?'

Mr Waite 'hurrumphed,' and for a moment I thought he was going to say 'no'. But to my surprise he agreed. I think he felt it would be one less boy to keep an eye on.

I went back to my desk, slipped my arms into my blazer sleeves, picked up my school cap and bicycle clips, and walked down the stone-floored hall to Mr Shaw's room to ask if my brother Tony could be allowed the same privilege.

Fifteen minutes later we sounded our bicycle bells as we approached the corner at the top of La Bellieuse, hugged the hedge as we turned into the lane, and pedalled up the drive to Wendy Cotte.

The bungalow already had a deserted look. All the windows were closed—even the circular air vents with their pear-shaped openings at the top of each frame had been shut—and all the curtains were drawn. Both the front door and the outer conservatory door were locked, the garage doors had been pushed together and bolted (which was rare) and the Vauxhall was neither parked in the driveway nor standing in the lane outside the house.

I peered through the crack between the ill-fitting garage doors, a cupped hand shading my eyes. 'I can see the window at the other end,' I mumbled, my lips against the wood. 'The car's not in there.'

'They must have gone,' Tony replied. He sounded despondent, discouraged.

'Already?'

'Well, they're not here! Are they?'

'But *we* haven't left yet. All the schools are supposed to go first.'

Tony shrugged. 'We could ask next door. Perhaps they'd know.'

But there was no response to our repeated knocks on the back door of the bungalow to the south, although some windows were open and the curtains were pulled back so we could see into the Millard's kitchen. Nor was there answer from the Taylor's bungalow to the north. The only signs of life came from the cages in our own garden, where the budgies still kept up their busy, noisy chatter.

Tony kicked disconsolately at the gravel as we walked back into our own driveway.

'No. It's good, really,' I said loudly, trying to sound cheerful. 'They'll be in England almost as soon as we are. You'll see.'

I started to run, heading round the side of the house. 'Come on,' I called, feeling I should add purpose to our visit. 'We're here anyway, we might as well feed the budgies. Let's get some seed from the farm.'

The previous evening my father had suggested I take my tin of budgie seed to La Douit farm and ask the Fromes to feed the birds.

'Just till I get back,' I said to the assembled Frome family—they were eating their supper—and plonked the remainder of my pocket money onto their kitchen table. 'That's so you can buy more seed.'

Mrs Frome put her hand over the coins and slid them back toward me. 'You keep that,' she said gently. For a moment I thought she was going to cry. 'You may need it where you're going.'

Now we ran past the silent dog run and empty chicken cages, climbed the earth bank at the foot of the garden and slid on our heels down the far side. We skirted round the edge of Mr Frome's upper field, where two tan-and-white Guernsey cows pulled at tufts of grass in their noisy, rasping way. Their heads were bent low but each kept a mournful, unblinking dark-brown eye turned in our direction.

At the foot of the field we turned into the thick-hedged track that led down to the Frome farmhouse, stepping nimbly over the cow patches that littered our route. Chickens scattered ahead of us, breaking into an awkward, encumbered run and occasionally flapping their wings and uttering squawks of protest.

The Fromes lived in a long two-storey house with 20-inch thick granite walls. Its windows were set deep within the walls, as was the Dutch door that opened onto the farmyard. Much of the house was covered with ivy that climbed all the way up the walls, reached searching tendrils onto the stone-tiled roof, and crept enquiringly up the chimney stack.

The upper half of the Dutch door was open and there stood our father! He was leaning on the shelf and talking to Mr Frome. They were so engrossed in their conversation that neither noticed us run into the yard.

'We thought you'd left!' Tony shouted, running breathlessly up to them.

'No, no. Not yet!' our father looked surprised. 'We thought *you* had gone.' He stepped back so that Mr Frome could open the lower half of the door.

He said that he and our mother had been asked to accompany one of the girls' schools, and were to be there at 7 p.m. They had hurriedly packed two suitcases and a few personal belongings, and piled them into the car, and locked up the house. 'Then,' he explained, his hand on his hips, 'there's your mother standing in the middle of the drive saying: 'Stan: I'm not leaving all our food for some rotten Jerries!''

We laughed: he had exactly mimicked her stance and tone.

'So you brought it here?' I asked.

'They certainly did,' Mr Frome replied, and he unlatched the lower half of the Dutch door and pushed it open.

'You'd better have some tea, seeing as you're here,' Mrs Frome commanded as her husband ushered us into the kitchen.

She placed her hands on our shoulders and steered us onto two chairs on the window side of the table. Our mother sat in a wooden armchair beside the unlit fireplace. Mrs Frome lifted the used plates and cups from in front of us and from a deal buffet standing against the wall took two willow-pattern tea plates and placed one in front of me and one in front of Tony, laying a bone-handled tea knife beside them. From the centre of the table she took a plate half-filled with buttered bread and held it in front of us in turn. 'We've had ours; your parents too. And there's more where that came from. Some of it's yours, anyway. So don't be afraid to tuck in.'

I stood at the Frome's gate and watched my father's black Vauxhall pull away from the front of La Douit farm and turn right toward St Martin's church. In the rear window I could see the pale shape of Tony's face and a hand waving beside it, both masked by alternate light and dark reflections on the glass as the car receded under the overhanging branches. I gave a cursory wave in return, turned, climbed over the wide timber gate and dropped into the farmyard.

I knew my father had been upset because I refused his offer to be driven back to the College. Tony had accepted readily, which made it even more difficult for me to say 'no.' I'd had to resort to excuses, first that I wanted to feed the budgies (and I held up a brown paper bag of seed I had ready), and then that I should really take my bike back to the College in case there was a delay before we left and I was needed as a messenger.

'Let him if he wants to, Stan,' my mother called across the top of the car. She opened the door on her side and climbed in. At such moments I knew I could depend on her to put a tight rein on her emotions and take a practical, no-nonsense stance. She would have been a tower of strength at Dunkirk.

My father stood irresolute for a moment and then bent down and pulled open the driver's door. 'You're sure?' he asked, still hesitating, his hand resting on its upper edge.

'Yes,' I replied. '*Yes!*' I smiled and nodded several times as if to urge my father to sit down.

How could I explain that I *savoured* being alone? That I needed a few private moments before I was thrown willy-nilly into communal living? While Mr Waite had been writing problems on the blackboard that morning, and the Fourth Form boys had been noisily scrambling to be the first with the correct answers, I had begun to perceive that we were embarking on a long term of regimented group living. I would be going to school with these 16 boys—and another 200 or so spread among the other Forms—not just for six or seven hours a day, but for twenty-four hours. I would be eating with them, playing games with them, washing with them, and sleeping with them, wherever the College was billeted. And unlike boys at other colleges in England, we would not be going home three times a year for holidays.

If the war went on for as long as the last one, I would have four years of living like that, day after day. Unless, in slightly less than three years—as soon as I was eighteen—I joined up. That would be one way of getting away. But would the army, or navy, or air force, be any better? Military life, I suspected, would see me bundled from place to place with a platoon of disgruntled privates. Unless, of course, belonging to the O.T.C. would bring me a commission: there might be a little more privacy if I were an officer. Really, I liked my original plan much better: to join the merchant navy as a wireless operator. Even if I had to sleep in a hammock with the ordinary seamen, at least I would have my private wireless cabin on the upper deck to work in.

As I crossed the wide courtyard between the house and farm buildings, I called 'Good bye' and 'Thank you' to the Fromes, both now standing inside the Dutch door leaning over the closed lower half. I retraced the path Tony and I had taken only an hour earlier and turned into the field that bordered the back garden of Wendy Cotte.

When I entered the budgies' cage the birds fluttered erratically. They swooped to one side of the cage, where they grasped the wire with curved talons and hung with their heads down and their tail feathers pointing up, and then they launched into a swift three-beat flight to the wire on the opposite side. I wondered momentarily whether their fussing was a sign of their affection for me, or simply that they were hungry. Probably the latter!

I reached into the shoulder-high dish on the far wall and stirred the old seed with my finger. Closing my eyes, I blew at the husks that had risen to the surface, feeling them brush against my cheeks and into my nose as they flew by. I had brought more seed than I really needed, and the excess spilled onto my shoes and bounced farther out onto the concrete floor. Immediately, the older, braver birds dropped vertically to the floor and started pecking at the seeds farthest from me.

As I closed the cage door I could hear muted voices and light steps on the gravel, coming from the front of the house. I wondered if my parents had come back for something, or if they had visitors. Both seemed unlikely.

I walked round the north side of the house, very quietly opening and closing the small gate set into the privet hedge. At first I could see no one, but the voices continued. I eased farther forward, keeping my feet silent by stepping on the stunted weeds that grew in the gravelled driveway. As I drew level with the front of the house I could see a man and woman leaning against the glass of my parents' bedroom window, their arms raised over their foreheads to deflect reflections.

'Are you looking for someone?' I asked.

The intruders leaped backward. I didn't know either of them, although the woman's face seemed familiar. Perhaps I had seen her in one of the shops, probably de Bertrands up by the church.

'Do you want something?' I repeated, standing about five feet from them.

'No, no!' the man replied quickly. Already he was shuffling sideways toward the rose arch. 'We…we just wanted to make sure…'

'That everything is secure,' the woman chimed in, unintentionally poetic. 'We're just keeping an eye on things. Er – for the owners.'

'Oh?' I replied quickly. 'There's no need to. Really. The family's staying, you see.'

'Well…that's all right, then,' the man muttered. They were in the driveway now, by the entrance, backing toward the lane.

I doubted that my parents would ask anyone other than their immediate neighbours, or more likely the Fromes, to 'keep an eye on things' at Wendy Cotte.

Is this what it's going to be like? I pondered. *Will those who leave have their homes plundered? From the invading army I suppose that's to be expected: it will be unwelcome, but empty dwellings are fair game. But from the islanders? And so soon?*

I wondered what to do with Tony's bike. I could hardly leave it resting against the garage wall, visible to the road, yet neither could I put it into the garage or the conservatory: the doors were locked. And the keys: where were they? Had my parents left them with the Fromes for safekeeping? They hadn't said. Or had they taken them with them, for the return which—they were not to know then—would never materialize? So I wheeled the bike round the side of the bungalow and pushed it inside the now-empty dog house, resting it against one of the tea chests in which the dogs curled up to sleep. Then I walked all around the house, testing doors and windows, not quite sure why but feeling I should check everything again.

I spun the nearer pedal of my bike to the bottom of its arc, stepped on it with my left foot, and coasted down the slope into the lane. As the bike gathered speed I swung my leg over the saddle and pedalled up La Bellieuse toward Les Merriennes and the town.

There was little traffic on the winding roads. I freewheeled much of the way, rapidly down Les Merriennes and then more leisurely down the gentler slope of Ville-au-Roi. I did not consciously notice the features that would mean so much to me later; features that would recur at unexpected moments like still frames from a moving picture; frames that would provide the key to a lifelong restlessness that I would be unable to pin down until I returned to Guernsey—again alone, at the age of 62—and retraced my route from Wendy Cotte to the gates of Elizabeth College.

*

It was 1987 when I parked a rented Ford Fiesta in front of La Douit farm (although now it seemed to have become a guest house) and walked up a short, steep, narrow lane that led into the foot of La Bellieuse. My plan was to walk slowly up the incline to the bungalow, peek in the gate, and—if I felt brash enough—ask if I could walk around to the back of the house and look over the hedge into the field below. But as I drew level with the entrance—which now sported two white chest-high pillars, one on either side, where I had known the entrance only as an opening cut in a grass-covered earth bank—two boys of about nine and eleven cycled out chatting amiably. Ignoring the elderly man standing against the stone wall on the opposite side of the lane, they turned left and freewheeled down the hill toward the church, just as Tony and I had so often done nearly fifty years before.

I found myself turning abruptly away, memories flooding back, making my eyes smart. I felt drawn compulsively in the opposite direction, toward Les Merriennes. The granite wall on my left seemed unchanged: moss and small plants still grew in the grout between its grey stones, exactly as I remembered.

So did the foliage-topped grass and earth bank on my right, with yellow primroses embedded in it and pink honeysuckle hanging from long branches.

At the foot of Les Merriennes a stone house on the left still jutted into an unwary cyclist's path. Like a flash-camera image, I remembered leaning my bike to the right as I veered past the sharply angled promontory. I strode on, more images flashing momentarily into mind: the low earth banks on my left, along Rue Poudreuse; the wide steps that let up to the post office at the top of Ville au Roi; the moss-patched granite walls on both sides of Queen's Road, the leafy branches of the tall beech trees rooted in the gardens behind them meeting overhead; the stately houses on both sides of The Grange, glass panels above their front doors declaring their owners' backgrounds: *Ladymeade; Espérance; Pres de L'Eglise; Verdun; Etretat; Brockhurst.*

I stood between Elizabeth College's wrought-iron gates, remembering the slithering crunch of loose gravel sliding under my wheels when, as a boy of 15, I occasionally turned too fast off the steep main road and skidded into the railings.

Only then did I recognize that these images, which had sprung infrequently but unexpectedly into mind at random intervals over the intervening years, emanated from that last, lonely ride; a ride that closed the book on my fifteenth year as a Guernsey resident.

12

20th June 1940: Evening

'It's my guess we'll be going on the *St Helier*,' said Willoughby. The *St Helier* was one of the red-funnelled passenger vessels that plied between Weymouth, Guernsey and Jersey.

'No. I bet it'll be the *Isle of Sark*,' another boy ventured.

'Can't be,' Luxton announced authoritatively. 'The *Isle of Sark* was due to dock at six this morning.' Luxton believed that if you said something assertively enough it became a fact. He was rarely challenged.

They were standing in the late evening dusk on the sea wall that ran the length of The White Rock: the main harbour wall jutting out from the foot of St Julian's Avenue. The Clock Tower atop the Weighbridge was behind them, and the two deep-water jetties where the cross-channel mailboats berthed were a hundred yards farther ahead.

An hour and a half earlier—shortly after 9 p.m.—the 227 boys had wound their way caterpillar fashion out of the College gates and down the long incline to the harbour, under the majestic trees that lined both sides of St Julian's Avenue. Each boy carried a suitcase in one hand and a bag of food in the other. A satchel of school books straddled each back and a square gasmask box, with its long string slung over one shoulder, bumped against the opposite hip.

They had completed a half circle round the periphery of St James's Church, crossed the steeply inclined road leading from Candie Gardens, sniffed the pungent smell from Randall's Brewery half way down the hill, and snaked past the now-closed Gaumont Cinema, taking quick peeks at the posters that advertised ***Untamed*** ('A Terrific Drama of the Far North, with Ray Milland and Akim Tamiroff') and ***Married and In Love*** ('Wife v. Glamour Girl in a Super Romantic Drama') which until the day before had been running as a double feature.

The infrequent traffic along the Esplanade halted while the 227 boys straggled across to the Weighbridge and up the four stone steps onto the granite sea wall, their suitcases, which had seemed to grow heavier as they marched down the hill, banging uncomfortably against their knees. The march had ended about two-thirds along the wall, where the boys were now bunched three-deep, their grey flannel suits, navy blue mackintoshes, and blue caps with white piping denoting where they stood. Farther along they could see the navy blue caps of the Boys' Intermediate, each with a fleck of yellow, green, blue, or red set into the quadrant just above the peak, denoting whether they belonged to the Mesny, Dorey, Blicq, or de Carteret House.

Now they watched children from more distant schools clambering out of buses and being marshalled in groups along the wide footpath on the seaward side of The Esplanade between the Weighbridge and the

Town Church. Dark green skirts and blazers showed where the Ladies College had assembled just beyond The Weighbridge.

I had groaned inwardly when my mother had handed me a string bag with a loop handle at the top, within it a paper bag containing a food pack wrapped in greaseproof paper, and had silently resolved to 'lose' the outer string covering, so my pack would be more like those the other Fourth Form boys undoubtedly would carry. Now I recognised my mother's forethought: the bag was easier to carry than just a paper bag, and it did not tear apart as some boys' already were doing. The unfortunate youths were now cramming buns, sandwiches, apples, tomatoes, chunks of cheese, and slices of gâche into their blazer and mackintosh pockets.

'What'd your mother give you to eat?' I heard one boy ask.

'Cheese and cucumber sandwiches, mostly. And a package of dates. What about you?'

'Tomato sandwiches. Tons of them.'

'Your father's a grower. What else do you expect!'

'D'you know what tomato sandwiches are like when you've been carrying them all day?' He opened a damp-looking paper bag and held it out for the other boys to peer into. 'Mush!'

Even the greaseproof paper wrapped around each pair of sandwiches had failed to contain the incipient seepage.

'My mum thought of that,' a freckle-faced boy with a stubby turned-up nose exclaimed. 'She made me and my sister ham sandwiches and gave us both a tin of fruit.' He held it up. 'Cling Peaches,' he read.

'Did you bring a tin opener?'

''Course!' the boy responded scornfully, patting his pocket. 'And a spoon.'

'Can I sit next to you, when they tell us we can eat? Swap some of my Christmas cake for some of your peaches?'

'Christmas cake? In June?'

'My mother always keeps one cake till the next year. Says it improves with age. She cut it last night: we all had a piece. Said there's no way she's going to leave *her* Christmas cake for a bunch of rotten Nazis!'

'Fair swap,' the boy bearing the tin of peaches responded. 'But I wish they'd let us eat. It's bloody heavy.' He glanced around furtively, fearing a Master might have heard him swear.

But the nearest Master—it was Mr Waite—was pre-occupied with a twelve-year old standing directly in front of him, and the youngster was looking up at him with a distressed expression.

'Sir! I need to go to the WC.'

'Did you not go before you left the College, boy?'

'Yes, sir. But…'

'Do you wish to urinate or defecate?' Mr Waite was well-known for his irony and for playing with long words. The Fourth Form boys were accustomed to him; the twelve-year-old was not.

'Sir?'

'Number One or Number Two, boy?'

The young boy shook his head blankly. He looked as if he might burst into tears.

'Do you need to stand up when you do it, or sit down?' Mr Waite's words were gentler now.

'Sit down, sir.'

'Oh, Lord!' Mr Waite looked around. 'Mr Pauls,' he called. 'Keep an eye on this unruly bunch for me; would you mind?' and he led the unhappy twelve-year-old down the steps toward the jetty.

'Are your parents leaving, too?' The question had been aired many times during the day.

'Yes. My father phoned my uncle last night. He lives in Coventry. They'll be going there. What about yours?'

'Dunno, really. My father says he can't just shut up the shop and leave, he's got his customers to think of. He wants my mother to go to my auntie's in Portsmouth. It's her sister, actually. But she says she won't go if he doesn't.'

'Mine are staying,' a third boy piped up. 'My dad thinks it's all a false alarm. We'll be back within a month.'

''Fraid not, old scout.' This was said by one of the prefects. 'I'm afraid it'll be…' He had been about to say *at least a year*, but changed it to: '…longer than that.'

In the gathering dusk a ship had slipped unnoticed into the Southern Railways berth on the far side of the New Jetty, all but the top of its mast hidden by the buildings on the pier. The children who had been clustered at the farthest end of the sea wall detached themselves from the main group and, led by a tall teacher carrying a walking cane as if it was an army officer's swagger stick, snaked their way down the four steps and across the road. They disappeared from view behind the administration buildings at the entrance to the jetty.

George Luxton was right: it was not the Isle of Sark. But neither was it any of the five other passenger boats the boys knew. This one seemed smaller than the average mailboat and had a much more bedraggled appearance. Even its superstructure looked grey.

A single gangplank with a rope on either side led up to an opening in the ship's railing. The boys struggled awkwardly up the steep incline, their suitcases, satchels and gas masks snagging the side ropes and their feet tripping on the treads. Strong seamen's arms pulled them onto a grey metal deck and steered them toward a set of steep stairs that seemed to descend deep into the bowels of the ship.

A deckhand grabbed each boy's suitcase and threw it down to another deckhand on a lower level, who handed it to the boy as he stepped onto the deck.

'Omkeren! Omkeren!' the deckhand at the top shouted, and gestured that the boys should turn around and go *backwards* down the stairs as if they were descending a ladder. If a boy still did not understand, the seaman grasped him by the shoulders and twisted him around.

'I think they're Dutch!' Smythe whispered to Collishawe as he put his foot on the deck below.

'I think you're right. The boat's called the *Batavier IV*. I saw it on a lifebelt.' Ships' identifications were supposed to have been removed from the bow and stern as a wartime security measure, but details like these were sometimes missed.

Still another seaman steered them to a second set of steps, and then a third. They descended deeper and deeper into the bowels of the ship. At the bottom they saw a wide, low-ceilinged cavern stretching ahead of them, a cavern that narrowed to a blunt point at the ship's bow. The shallow openness was interrupted by three rows of dark steel pillars with rings embedded in them about three feet above the deck. The ceiling was low and had rows of knobble-headed rivets running both fore and aft and athwart the ship's beam. Naked incandescent bulbs, each protected by a heavy wire cage, were clamped to the pillars. Four concave channels were set into the deck running across the ship, and a single, wider channel ran fore and aft.

'It's a cattle ship!' announced Girouard, whose father had something to do with one of the shipping lines that plied between the islands. 'You can tell by the troughs in the floor.'

'Deck,' Luxton corrected him.

'Cor! You certainly can tell!' This was Collishawe. 'What a pong!' And he pinched his nose.

'Come on you boys! Move along!' The military-minded teacher apparently had assumed command. He pointed to two rows of pillars along the starboard side of the ship: 'Intermediate School, in those two rows.' He pointed to two rows of pillars down the centre: 'Elizabeth College, between these pillars.'

The boys shuffled along until they had formed a straggly line, and then unslung their satchels and dropped them onto the deck.

'You College boys will have to move closer to each other than that,' the teacher called out after they had sat down. 'Take just enough room so you can stretch out comfortably.'

'Comfortably!' Tostevin Junior echoed, patting the rough grey steel as they shuffled farther along on their knees. 'On this soft surface?'

'Like sardines in a tin!' Martin stage-whispered.

'Glad he's not one of our teachers,' somebody replied. 'He makes me feel like *I'm* cattle.'

'Did you see the scars on the deck?' Martin asked, his mouth full of cheese sandwich. At last they had been given permission to eat.

'She's been shot at somewhere,' George Luxton announced.

'There's a big hole in the funnel,' another boy commented.

'Toward the back, about half way up,' a fourth boy called from one of the Intermediate School rows. 'And one of the lifeboats on the far side is smashed.'

'That's the starboard,' Luxton added between bites. But even he did not know that the *Batavier IV* had been sent to Guernsey immediately after rescuing British troops from the Dunkirk beaches.

The cattle ship had put to sea half an hour ago, its departure signalled by the vibration of the engines and the throb of the screw. There was little sea motion but the waves could be heard splashing against the steel plates that separated the boys from the sea.

'Are we below sea level, sir?' a nervous younger boy asked one of the Masters.

'Oh, I doubt it,' he responded cheerfully. 'You wouldn't hear the waves if you were below water level. Would you?'

'No, sir. I suppose not.'

'But there aren't any portholes, sir!' This was Le Poidevin.

'I don't think cargo boats really have portholes. Do you?' The Master had taken up a position squatting cross-legged on the deck among the boys and, like them, was munching on sandwiches his wife had prepared for him. 'Except the crew,' he added. 'And their quarters are usually on an upper deck.'

Although he was displaying a relaxed *laissez-faire* demeanour to the boys around him, I suspected that privately he was worrying what his wife had been able to arrange and whether she would have an opportunity to leave before German troops arrived.

'Can we go up on deck, sir? Have a gander?'

'I'm afraid not. No one is allowed on deck.'

The *Batavier IV* started to pitch and roll mildly as it pulled away from the islands and headed north into mid-Channel. It was not yet enough to cause queasiness, but sufficient for me to realize that a strong wind and unruly sea could create tremendous problems. Proper lavatories were non-existent. The only facilities were an eight-foot trough that served as a urinal and three buckets behind a partition at the rearward end of the deck. The unventilated area had already become too warm for comfort, and that, combined with the previous cattle smell (or was it the residue of the Dunkirk evacuation?), would be enough to test even the most robust constitution.

I hardly dared conjecture the effect of seven or eight hundred children regurgitating their meals onto the deck around them—the cream buns, fruit, gâche, tomatoes, Christmas cake, tinned peaches, and even chocolate éclairs that some mothers had packed in mistaken gestures of affection.

I lay on my back, staring up at the riveted steel plates protruding from the bulkhead above. I had tried lying first on one side and then on the other, but the steel deck pressing relentlessly onto my hip and shoulders had proved far too uncomfortable. I had tried willing myself to sleep, but it hadn't worked. I couldn't stop my mind from roving, from reliving the events of the past thirty-six hours, from projecting forward to the unknown.

Intruding into what I had so far regarded as an adventure, like something from a Percy Westerman story, was the realization that Wendy Cotte—the home we had moved into with my parents when I was one year old—was standing forlorn, possibly even desecrated. And the five members of my family were scattered, going to separate, unnamed destinations: the children to one, the parents to another.

I sensed that my brothers and I would be secure, no matter where we were. *(How fortunate*, I thought, *that I won a scholarship so we could all be at the same school.)* The College would be lodged somewhere by 'the authorities'—whoever was organizing the move—so it would remain as an independent entity that the boys could identify with, and its Masters would provide the nurturing that some of the younger boys

In the hold of the Batavier IV

would need. It was my parents I was more worried about: not only had they made a momentous decision to give up everything they owned, but also they would become displaced persons, homeless and nearly penniless, for my father wouldn't have a job and they could not take much money from the bank because everyone was trying to do the same. I wondered whether their decision had been made too hurriedly, that perhaps they should have stayed behind so my father could keep on working. But no, I knew his philosophy, his determination. He may have appeared to be a mild man who hated to ruffle the surface or cause a fuss, yet deep, deep down I knew he would resist vehemently taking orders from an occupying commander on what he could and could not print. No. His life would be more secure this way.

A hand was shaking my shoulder. I must have dozed off.

'Are you awake?' It was Tony, kneeling on the floor in the narrow space between me and Frank Sarre's supine form, curled into a neat 'S'. Frank's athletic yet compact frame always managed to look tidy.

'Are you awake?'

I pushed myself up on one elbow, remembering my father's exhortations to keep an eye open for my brothers. My left hip and shoulder were sore from the hard deck and my neck felt twisted and stiff from having slipped off my mackintosh, which I had folded to form a sort-of pillow. Around me were rows of huddled figures in similar uncomfortable positions. Nearly all the boys slept, except for a handful staring blankly up at the lamp bulbs above them, and three who were huddled over the trough and were making excruciating noises. Two more pale-faced boys with their hands over their mouths were making their way queasily toward the trough. The heat was unbearable—I was sweating profusely—and the stench was awful.

At three a.m. I had sensed a change in engine sound and that the ship was rolling considerably: a slow, insidious roll that was much more disturbing than the sharper, more clearly defined roll we had experienced earlier; a roll that caused the procession of boys to the trough. (A few had wakened too late and had unhappily deposited their souring lunches beside their sleeping positions, to the dismay of their neighbours and unspoken chagrin of their Masters.) The engines were beating faster now and the roll was less noticeable.

'There was an explosion,' Tony was saying.

I sat up further. 'An explosion?'

Tony nodded. 'About twenty minutes ago.'

'Oh, I don't think so, Tony. You must have dreamt it.' I stretched out my wrist and glanced at the hands of my watch: it was 4:45. 'Go back to your spot. Try to sleep some more.'

'No.' Tony was shaking his head. 'That's just it. I couldn't sleep, so I went on deck…'

'Nobody's allowed on deck.'

'Well, I went. It was so hot and smelly.' He wrinkled his nose. 'I couldn't bear it any longer. All the Masters were asleep or…somewhere. David Martel will tell you. He went up too. But he didn't stay. He didn't take a pullover with him and he found it was too cold.'

'But I'd have heard an explosion…,' I tried to explain. 'We all would.'

'No, no! Not on this ship. On another one.'

'Another one?'

'Yes. In front of this one, to the left. Quite a long way. It was just getting light.'

'Are you sure?'

'Yes.' Tony nodded his head vigorously. 'There was a flash, like big flames, and a few seconds later a sort of boom, like thunder.'

'You actually saw it?'

'That's why I came down. I didn't like it.'

Mr Shaw was approaching, a little unsteadily, stepping between the sleeping boys and treading carefully, balancing himself with each roll of the ship.

'Are you all right?' He looked at Tony.

Tony started to stand up.

'No. Don't get up.'

'I was talking to my brother, sir.'

'I see.' He paused, then added almost as an afterthought: 'I couldn't see you, a little while ago….'

'I couldn't sleep, sir.'

'Well, be sure to tell me another time. So I know where you are.'

'Sorry, sir.'

Mr Shaw turned away and started to thread his way back.

Tony whispered: 'I'd better go with him,' and he crept after the receding figure.

I lay back on my makeshift pillow, trying to ignore the ugly sounds and smells around me. *Had Tony really seen an explosion? Or had he been dreaming?* Tony was much more sensitive and imaginative than I was. He could well have imagined the whole sequence, in the half light between sleeping and waking. But…it was wartime and, well, possible. Before drifting into a light sleep I resolved to ask David Martel if Tony and he had really been on deck. That should provide an answer.

But it didn't, because David was with the Boys Intermediate and his school went to a different destination the next day. (It was a full decade before I met David again. Long before then my father told me that he had gone into the *Guernsey Press* office the following morning and had read on the Creed machine that the Luftwaffe had dropped six mines in the English Channel outside the Portland Naval Centre, which was adjacent to the *Batavier IV*'s destination. During the night minesweepers found five of the mines, but not the sixth. Coded messages were radioed to the *Batavier IV* and other ships that were headed toward the port, instructing them to sail parallel to the coast until they were called in. This had accounted for the *Batavier IV's* reduced speed and wallowing roll. But as dawn approached and the sixth mine still had not been found, it was considered less risky to have the ships turn toward the port and chance encountering the mine, than leave them as 'sitting ducks' in full daylight in the English Channel where they would be ready prey for marauding E-boats and fighter-bombers.)

The *Batavier IV* was sailing north, close in to the shore, before its passengers were allowed on deck. The schools were still segregated, with the boys on the foredeck and the girls, who had been in the cattle pens at the rear of the ship, behind the funnel. Ahead of the ship, about a mile away and twenty degrees off the port bow, was a promontory of land with a cliff-like hill rising to some three or four hundred feet, on which banks of row houses were set with windows that peered into their neighbours' chimney pots. At the farthest extremity to the left was flatter land with a lighthouse and, on the shore, jagged, vertical rocks against which waves beat in a soft summer swell. Ahead and slightly to their right were beaches with single houses sprinkled behind them among stretches of pastoral land.

They seemed to be sailing into the left-hand side of a large bay with grayish-white cliffs rising intermittently to the right as far as the schoolboys could see. The raised prow at the front of the *Batavier IV* prevented them from seeing directly ahead.

'It doesn't look like Southampton, does it?' a boy asked.

Boys of Elizabeth College and the Boys Intermediate on the foredeck of Batavier IV as the ship sails into Weymouth Harbour. Photo by Anthony Blicq (the photo is a contact print and the only existing copy).

'No,' Collishawe replied. 'We'd be in the Solent and you'd be able to see the Isle of Wight.'

'More like Dover, I should think.' That was Beauchamp. 'You can tell by the cliffs.'

At first no one thought to challenge him. Keith Beauchamp's parents lived in Canterbury, which wasn't all that far from Dover, so he would know.

But somehow the cliffs didn't look right, not like the pictures they had seen in their geography books. They weren't as white and they didn't seem as tall or as steep, although it was difficult to tell at that distance.

'Why would we be going to Dover?' Franklin asked, his black curls stiffened and unruly, pushing up the front of his cap.

'We could be going round Dover to Gravesend,' Beauchamp explained, 'or right into London.'

'Then the cliffs would be on our left, not our right,' Collishawe rationalized. 'I've an idea it's Weymouth.'

'Don't think so,' the boy put in. 'I can't see the docks.'

Collishawe appealed to one of the Masters: 'What do you think, sir?' he called to Mr Chambers, who taught Chemistry.,

'Well? What *do* I think?'

'Sorry, sir! I thought you'd heard. We wouldn't be going into Weymouth, would we?'

'It's Weymouth, all right,' Mr Chambers replied. 'You're seeing it from a different angle. We're coming in a bit from the west, around Portland Bill. You can see the lighthouse over there, on the left. When we're a bit farther round you'll see the town, behind the hill.'

13

21st June to 10th July 1940

Weymouth—normally a summer seaside resort, populated even in wartime by a scattering of holidaymakers—offered the evacuees a hot, tiring, and boring day. They were led into a theatre on the pier, where in previous summers stand-up comedians like Nosmo King and tenors singing Irish ballads such as 'Danny Boy' had provided revue-type entertainment for not very discriminating audiences. Today the boys and girls of Guernsey's schools sat in rows, waiting: waiting to be fed; waiting to be taken to the WC; waiting to be taken to a screened lobby for a medical inspection, where they suffered the indignities of having their hair searched for lice; waiting to be 'documented,' which meant giving their name, address, date and place of birth, age, sex, school, and names and birthplaces of parents; waiting for a luggage label with their name, age, and school hand-printed on it, to be tied through the buttonhole of their blazer; and finally waiting to find out where they would be going. They were not told, and neither were their teachers.

At dusk they climbed into tired-looking carriages of a dusty train that had pulled into Weymouth Quay, where in previous years the Great Western Railway's fast, elegant, *Paddington—Channel Islands Boat Train* had whistled importantly on its twice-daily run into the quayside station. When at last the makeshift arrangement of coaches had been filled and the train steamed out, the boys chortled on seeing that their train was running down the centre of the road between houses, pubs, and small businesses. They waved at passers-by, who waved back at them as if they were a school outing, unaware of the extraordinary purpose of their journey. Then night fell, and the boys of Elizabeth College settled down for a second night's uncomfortable sleep, many on the floor, which they claimed was eminently sweeter and softer than the steel floor of the previous night.

They awoke in a silent train parked in a grey, dingy railway station. Throughout the night they had been aware of extended periods of travel separated by long silences while they stood in a siding or small station, then shunting as they seemed to be moved from one section of track to another. Even the boys sitting against the windows could not peek out because the blinds had to be kept shut as part of the country's blackout regulations. They supposed they were at their destination, but could not identify it because the railway station's name had been obliterated from signboards and posters.

Johnson lowered a window and called out to a porter on the station platform. 'Where are we, sir?'

'Oldham, lad.'

'Oldham?' The name meant nothing to him.

'Aye. You heard owt?'

He shook his head.

'You know where Lancashire is?'

Johnson nodded.

'Then that's it.'

The Elizabeth College boys filed down the platform carrying their luggage, books, and gas masks—but now without sandwich bags—and scrambled up the steps onto the bridge that crossed over the railway tracks. They were packed into buses and driven to the centre of the town, where they lugged their belongings up five flights of stairs to the attic above a department store.

For the next three weeks they slept on straw-filled mattress-covers laid in rows on the floor, with naked rafters above them angled across the roof. They were taken out for walks in long, winding lines through the narrow, grey streets, returning for meals in a hastily set-up cafeteria in the employees' rest area. And on every third day they were marched to the public baths, not to swim but to clean themselves.

On the eighteenth day the Headmaster stood in front of his 227 boys, who squatted in tight rows on the floor of the crowded attic. 'Arrangements have been made for the College to be billeted in a permanent residence at Great Hucklow in Derbyshire,' he said. 'That's in hilly country about twelve miles from Buxton. It won't be quite like Guernsey, but at least you won't be in an industrial city.'

Nobody seemed to have heard of Great Hucklow, or Buxton even, but it sounded large and countryish so the boys took heart and looked forward to the change. They were tired of the regimented life imposed upon them in the tight quarters of the attic, and of the greyness and dustiness of industrial Lancashire, where a sunny day offered only limp, smoke-hazy rays glanced between near-black buildings.

Two days before Elizabeth College was to leave Oldham, I asked Mr Waite for permission to try to find my parents. My father had said they would be accompanying one of the girls' schools that would be travelling a day or two later than we had, and by adroitly questioning the men and women who seemed to be arranging the College's meals and bathing facilities, I had been told that most girls' schools were billeted in Rochdale, and it was easy to get to. The name Rochdale was familiar to me, because that was where singer Gracie Fields came from.

Mr Waite conferred with the Headmaster, who to my surprise said I could go the following day.

'But how do you propose to get there?' Mr Waite asked.

'By bus, sir. I asked the woman in the kiosk at The Baths. She said it's only about eleven miles, over the hill. And I'll ask my way as I go.'

'All right, then. But you *must* be back by six p.m. You must promise me that.'

'Yes, sir.'

'Very well. Go right after breakfast. And eat a good one. You may need it!'

'Thank you, sir. Yes, I will.' I was about to turn away, but Mr Waite stopped me.

'Do you…ummm…do you have any money?'

'Yes, sir. My father gave me some before we left.'

'Enough to get there and back?'

'Yes, sir. I'm sure.'

I felt less sure than I let Mr Waite see. I had no map and only one shilling and tenpence remaining of the five shillings my father had given each of us before we left Guernsey. But I could never ask a Master for money.

I sought Tony and Ian out and explained that I wouldn't be there the next day and told them what I planned to do. They both clamoured to be allowed to go with me, so they too could see their parents, and couldn't understand why it was acceptable for me to go but not for them. Yet, much as I would have appreciated their company, I sensed intuitively that travelling alone would be much simpler. I would be able to move faster and it would be much less expensive. I'd have to search for toilets less often (I seemed to have an extraordinarily strong bladder whereas Tony, because of an operation he had when he was 11, had to stop far more often). And I would have to cope with only one person's weariness: mine.

Nevertheless, I viewed the journey with some concern, suddenly aware that living in Guernsey had given me only a very limited knowledge of the wider world I was about to encounter, a world all too familiar to boys my own age who had grown up on the mainland. My only, very rudimentary, knowledge came from reading books and seeing the occasional (mostly American) film. Today, Guernsey children are much more worldly wise, even if they have not travelled outside the island, through watching television.

I slept fitfully, determined to be up early and first in line for the bathroom and then breakfast. I brushed my teeth peremptorily, washed quickly, and ran a wet comb through my hair, thankful we had been to the baths the day before and it was still soft and manageable. I sensed that to arrive with a neat appearance would go a long way toward convincing my parents that my brothers were well cared for.

From the department store I walked east, toward a road I had seen during the College's walks, a main road with numerous bus stops. 'Please, can you tell me where I should stand to catch a bus going toward Rochdale?' I asked a grey-haired man standing at the end of the line of the first bus queue I encountered.

'On t'other side, lad.' He pointed to a queue across the road. 'Over yon. You'll be wanting a number seventeen, I reckon.'

Ten minutes later I felt elated: not only had I started the journey quickly, but I had overcome the unexpected nervousness—the aloneness—I had suddenly experienced on leaving the familiar shelter of the department store attic and the unspoken moral support of my school friends. When I stepped alone into the street I had been concerned that I might not be able to find the way and would have to turn back, or I might not have the nerve to approach strangers to ask for direction, or they might not understand me or even be unwilling to help. It had not occurred to me that the white evacuee identification label tied to my blazer would soften people's reaction to me.

Now I *knew* I was going to find my parents. And here I was, for the first time in my life, riding atop a double-decker bus, sitting right up front! An impossibility in Guernsey, where the roads were so narrow the island had to order specially built short, single-deck narrow buses.

But after some kindly but misinformed help, two changes of bus, and a lengthy journey in the wrong direction, my exhilaration ebbed in tandem with a gnawing feeling in the pit of my stomach—I had not thought to ask for a pack lunch at breakfast. And the journey from Oldham to Rochdale seemed to be taking much longer than I had expected. (That a train would have been a faster and much simpler way to travel had not occurred to me: I was accustomed to buses and thought that was the way everyone travelled in England.)

Three rides later (on the last of which the conductor had let me ride without paying, for I had only two pennies rubbing against one another in my pocket and the fare was threepence-halfpenny), I followed the bus conductor's advice and jumped off the rear platform in front of a red-brick church. As I walked up a short gravelled path, I was surrounded by girls roughly my own age, all from the north end of the island, each with a label tied to a blazer or blouse button. They plied me with questions: *Where are you billeted? What's Oldham like? Are there any other schools there?*

I said I knew only about Elizabeth College, and anyway we would be moving up to Derbyshire the next day.

'Do you know Pierre Le Coq?' asked a dark-haired girl whose label declared she was Pierre's older sister.

'I saw him yesterday,' I said. 'He's all right. He's doing fine.'

I saw the furrows between her eyebrows soften. 'Tell him you saw me, will you?' She smiled and pointed to the label hanging from her blazer button. 'Pamela.'

I nodded and turned to answer another girl's question. And then another; and another. When they saw I had little to tell them, some of the girls began to drift away.

I turned back to Pamela: 'D'you know if my parents are here?'

She leaned forward to peer at my name.

'Yes,' she said, and inclined her head toward the far end of the church. 'They are here. In the office. With the teachers.'

I suddenly experienced an immense feeling of relief: not because I had found them, but because now I knew for certain they had been able to leave Guernsey too.

*

'We knew you had left Guernsey,' my father said, and pulled a folded newspaper clipping from his pocket. It was dated Thursday, 21st June.

A single-column headline announced:

THE EVACUATION

Beneath it a subhead proclaimed:

PROCEEDING REGULARLY AND RAPIDLY

I read on:

The evacuation of school children is continuing at full speed. There are never-to-be-forgotten scenes at the White Rock as more and more leave. Last evening the boys and girls of the Colleges and Intermediate Schools left in a large cargo boat.

Cheerfully and happily they marched to the quayside. School songs and popular community songs, interspersed, were shouted into the night air as the schools embarked…

'It wasn't quite like that,' I remarked, rather embarrassed. 'Quieter, I mean.'

In the early hours of the morning the remainder of the Primary School children embarked.

Later mothers and young children, many of them babies in arms, streamed on to the ships bravely trying to smile.

I knew who had written that piece—or overwritten it! My money would be on Nellie Emmett.

Many other islanders were crowding the mailboats; other children were embarking in cargo boats, crowding into cabins and holds.

It is estimated that to date, some
6,000 people have been evacuated.

'You know the island's occupied now?' my father asked.

'Yes,' I said. 'The headmaster announced it. On the 28th, I think.'

Without my desk calendar to change every morning, I had lost track of the date. And the repetitive eating, walking, washing, sleeping routine in Oldham had contributed a sameness to the days.

The calendar's five cubes will still be showing 20 6 40, I thought. *They always will, until I can go home and change them.* The realization occurred to me suddenly, irrevocably.

And then I remembered the man and woman whom I had seen peering into our windows after I had fed the budgies on that last evening, when I cycled away from Wendy Cotte for the last time. With a sinking feeling I wondered if my calendar was already announcing the date from someone else's desk or mantelpiece. And if someone else was winding up my Hornby clockwork train engine, or fingering the gilt on my coronation coach, or reading my treasured, special edition of *Treasure Island.*

I shivered slightly, trying to shove the thought away.

'It was tough for some of the boys,' I said. 'Especially for the younger ones whose parents had said they had to stay in Guernsey.'

Some of the boys had cried, and the Masters had to comfort them. It was sad, sort of embarrassing for them; both of them. I was only just beginning to understand how the boys must feel.

*

'We would have written to you,' my mother explained later, before I left to find my way back to the school. 'Will you tell Tony and Ian? We had no idea where you were.'

'It wouldn't have made any difference,' I said, 'because we're leaving Oldham tomorrow. That's what I came to tell you.' And I told them about Great Hucklow.

'Well, you may not stay there for long,' my father said. 'In another month we may be coming to fetch all three of you. We're thinking of going to Canada.'

*

Two days later seven tour buses carried the boys and Masters of Elizabeth College on a long drive into the green, fresh-smelling, rolling hills of Derbyshire and halted in a tiny village. Stretched along the two sides of a narrow, curved road, the boys could see about a dozen stone homes, a church, a pub, a shop-come-post office with a Cadbury's sign above its single window and, behind the church, the village hall: a low wood-construction building with a corrugated-iron roof.

'This is *Great* Hucklow?' Franklin observed from his seat at the front of the bus.

The bus driver said it was.

'Then I'd like to see how big *Little* Hucklow is!'

The older boys laughed.

The younger boys, their Masters, and six of the prefects stepped down from the first two buses and stood doubtfully in loose groups in front of the low building, which was to become their home 'for the duration'—an expression coined in 1940 to describe the uncertainty of evacuees' homeless plight.

The drivers of the five remaining buses engaged bottom gear and climbed slowly and noisily to the top of a steep winding hill. The driver of the front bus jumped out and opened a wide, narrow-barred white gate. The following buses bumped through it and along a rough two-lane track, drawing to a halt beside an empty aircraft hangar. A sign announced that until recently it had been the home of 'The Lancashire and Derbyshire Gliding Club.'

The hangar was to become the older boys' communal bedroom, and the club's buildings were to become the College's dining room and classrooms until more appropriate accommodation could be found.

*

Elizabeth College remained in Derbyshire until the end of the teaching year in the summer of 1945, with the younger boys resident in the Great Hucklow village hall. The older boys stayed in the cold, wind-blown hangars perched on the hill that overlooked the village until the autumn of 1940, then moved to Whitehall, a large private house three miles outside Buxton.

The younger boys progressed steadily through their school years, under the tutelage of the Masters and the personal guidance of both the Masters and the Masters' wives. Some of the older boys continued only until they were old enough to enlist, others finished their schooling in the Upper Sixth and then enlisted, while still others moved on to a university to continue their education.

The College now has three times the number of pupils it had in 1940, and enrols both male and female students. It also has an extensive summer school for students from the continent. The buildings look little different from when I attended the College sixty years ago—both inside and out. A noticeable difference is the gravel entranceway on which my bicycle's tires so often skidded when I exited off the slope of The Grange and turned in through the gates. The gravel has been replaced by smooth grey asphalt with parking lines painted on it, and all signs of the mounds above the air-raid trenches the older boys had cut into the stony ground in 1939 have been eliminated.

Postscript

What Happened to The Family?

My father's prognostication that we might be going to Canada 'for the duration' was correct: at the urging of my mother's now-Canadian brothers, Tony, Ian and I were withdrawn from Elizabeth College in Derbyshire and, on a grey, squally day in late July, the family boarded the Canadian Pacific liner *Duchess of Atholl* at its berth in Liverpool. The ship cast off from the dock and for the next seven days, with its sister ship *Duchess of Bedford* as a smudge on the horizon, beat a hasty but risky zig-zag course across the North Atlantic (zig-zagging to foil possible U-boat attacks) and docked in Montreal eight days later. For my parents, the final 24 hours as we sailed quietly down the St Lawrence River must have been a tremendous relief, for no longer was there any danger of torpedo attacks. They knew that our cabins on the lowest deck were below sea level and there would be little chance of escape if a U-boat launched a torpedo at the *Duchess of Atholl.*

We disembarked before 9 a.m. and discovered it would be another 12 hours before our train was scheduled to depart for Winnipeg, where Harold Steele, my mother's brother, would meet us and he and his family would help us get established. So, what should we do to fill in the time?

To escape the severe heat, for Montreal was experiencing a heat wave and we were dressed in British woollens, my father suggested to my mother we should go to a cinema. He could see a cinema across the street, its posters advertising it was ten degrees cooler inside.

'How many, please?' a young woman who was painting her nails behind a glassed-in booth window asked my father.

'Five. Two adults and three children.'

'I'm sorry, sir. No children.'

'*No children?*' My father was incredulous. He peered again at the films' posters to see if they contained material unsuitable for children, but neither did so. 'They're suitable for everybody!' he said.

'Not in Montreal. You'll have to go to Lachine if you want your children to go in with you.'

We were flabbergasted. We weren't to know then that a cinema fire several years earlier had killed over one hundred Montreal children, and since then Montreal law had prohibited attendance by anyone under 18.

Two tram rides later (we did not know yet they were called street cars) we were sitting in the balcony of a nearly empty cinema in Lachine, watching a double feature which none of us could remember afterwards. There is no doubt our minds, and particularly those of our parents, were elsewhere.

My father's thoughts, I know now, centred on the family's finances. Ever a cautious, prudent man, he must have been appalled that we had been able to bring so little money with us, and now that Guernsey was occupied territory he would have no access to any funds he still had in the Guernsey bank. Britain was besieged, both by an encroaching enemy and by a severe financial crisis. Consequently, travellers were allowed to take only £10 apiece out of the country, which meant that as a family we had only £50 between us, equivalent to about $225 in Canadian funds, and some of it had already been spent on the ship and in Montreal. More would be needed for meals during the two days we would be on the train. When we arrived in Winnipeg, he estimated we would be down to $180. He would have to get a job immediately.

*

The only discrepancy in the previous chapters was the presumption on my parents' part that they would be returning to Guernsey at the end of the war. Several factors deflected them from that objective, much to their dismay. The owners of the *Guernsey Press* chose not to hold my father's job open for him, claiming that his decision to leave the island in 1940 was equivalent to a resignation. Wendy Cotte, their beloved bungalow, had been occupied by German troops and had been severely damaged internally. Because no mortgage payments could be made while it was in occupied territory, after the war the house had to be sold, at a much depreciated value, to make up the deficiency. My parent's car, furniture and personal belongings also had disappeared, so they had nothing left of their past existence in Guernsey other than the clothing they had carried with them; like their children, they could each take just one suitcase.

In 1946 they wrote to friends in Guernsey and asked them to search the island for anything they could find. The friends shipped just a handful of items; in fact the remains of the family's belongings filled a box no more than 2 ft x 2 ft x 4 ft. Among them were: a three-foot sword case made in India from a young alligator, with the sword housed within the alligator's body and sheathed through the alligator's open mouth, that had belonged to my grandfather; a three-foot-high 'grandmother' clock that had been presented to my mother's parents on their 50th wedding anniversary; my mother's stamp album; two Indian lamp holders; a few spoons and embroidered doilies; a late 19th century soldier's dress helmet; and, incredibly, the air raid messenger's shrapnel helmet my mother had not allowed me to take to school on 20th June 1940!

In the five and a half years they had been in Canada, my parents had rented a three-bedroom house and filled it with an assortment of used furniture, aware they would part with most of their newly acquired belongings before they returned to Guernsey. Now they would have to start building a permanent collection of household goods.

*

What effect did the evacuation, and then the news that we would not be returning to Guernsey, have on each of us? And what subsequently happened to us, since 1945?

We were each affected differently, depending mostly on our age on arriving in Canada, and the events each of us faced during the ensuing years.

My Mother: Marjorie

In my mother's case, I think she was so caught up in the logistics of the evacuation that she was far less affected than my father. Throughout her life, until she came to Guernsey in 1921, she had been exposed to the army's practice of posting its staff periodically, and so had grown accustomed to pulling up stakes and setting up home in a new location every so many years. True, she had more difficulty than my father adapting to Canadian culture and informality, and wept copiously in 1946 when she and my father finally realized they could not, for physical, financial and emotional reasons, return to Guernsey. Yet she seemed to recover fairly quickly. She had no family or historical ties to the island and, although she loved Guernsey, she had no family members living there to add reason for her to return.

My mother was a great organizer and she and her father had been heavily involved in organizing and administering the St. John Ambulance brigade in Guernsey. So she sought out the St John Ambulance service in Winnipeg and became very active with them. She also started a mornings-only crêche for up to six local pre-schoolers in her and my father's home on Lanark Street. Both these activities helped shield her from the loss she and my father had experienced. She was *busy* right up until her unexpected death on Boxing Day in 1968, just before her 73rd birthday.

My Father: Stanley

For my father it was completely different. Although no 'Blicq' forbears were then living on the island (there were several cousins I discovered later, but he did not know about them, or they about him), he had a long heritage on his grandmother's side of the family. Before her marriage to John L'Ereaux, Priscilla had been a De Moulpied, a well-known family of landowners living at Le Variouf, and their history can be traced by examining the record of interments on the De Moulpied tomb beside St. Martin's Church, where she was buried in 1936.

My father had a strong sense of identity with his island, and had proudly represented Guernsey in the militia during the 1914-18 war, and in inter-island sport. He was also a very sensitive man, and privately a romanticist, though he rarely let that side of his character show. On the afternoon of 3rd September 1939, we as a family had sat in our living room listening to the wireless as Neville Chamberlain told us that, despite his government's efforts, Great Britain was again at war with Germany. The national anthem was played immediately after his announcement and we all stood stiffly at attention, facing inward toward each other (which at the time, in my inexperienced youth, I found faintly embarrassing). It was the glistening in my father's eye that most affected me, which at the time I put down to his recollecting his awful experiences in the 1914-18 war. It was not until much later that I realized he was thinking of his sons: if this new war lasted as long as the last one, his eldest son certainly would be caught up in it. That, too, was a contributing factor in wanting his sons to leave the island: he feared that as soon as they became old enough to enlist, they would be carted off to an internment camp in Germany.

Having to take his dogs to be destroyed completely devastated him. They were his pride and his pleasure; his major outlet from the pressures of work and marriage. Yet, in his characteristic way, he did not allow his grief to surface in front of his family, although I sensed subliminally how much he must be grieving for them.

He suffered immense personal guilt, partly about his dogs and partly because he felt he was shirking his responsibility as editor of the *Guernsey Press*. For all that he claimed that he could not 'work under the Jerries,' he also felt he was deserting the *Press* and his island at the time of their greatest need.

Within a week of the family's arrival in Winnipeg he secured a position as a copy editor at the *Winnipeg Free Press*, remaining with them for 23 years until his retirement in 1963. In 1942, realizing there was no children's magazine in Canada, he started publishing *Canada's Own Children's Newspaper* as a sideline. It was a 16-page tabloid-size and he published it privately for five years. It was a significantly non-profit activity (it was distributed free to schools and children-oriented organizations), written and edited by my father, who also did his own marketing and persuaded Winnipeg businesses to place advertisements in it, to help defray the cost.

Surprisingly, my parents chose not to return to Guernsey, even for a visit, and in fact never travelled outside the Province of Manitoba, despite their sons' frequent exhortations that they should do so. Instead, every summer they drove 150 miles northwest of Winnipeg to Wasagaming in Riding Mountain National Park, for a two-week holiday beside Clear Lake. My mother would have been open to wider travel, but my father seemed to have become almost reclusive, afraid to jolt the blanket of security he had rebuilt around him. He died at the age of 82, in 1975.

The Three Brothers

Anthony (Tony)

Of the three brothers, Tony was most affected by the evacuation. Although his parents recognized it only marginally, he was in fact very artistic and had a temperament to accompany it: consequently his feelings were much nearer the surface than those of his brothers.

To each of us in turn, as we neared graduation from high school, our security-minded father had given the same advice: 'Try to get a job in the civil service, or in a bank, or as a teacher. That way you will have a secure career and you will be reasonably well paid.' For someone who had lived through the depression years of the 1930s, that seemed like a sound guideline.

So, when Tony graduated from high school in the summer of 1943 at the age of 16 (because of the more accelerated British education system, Tony and I were an average 16 months younger than our Canadian peers), he obtained a junior accounting position with the Province of Manitoba Department of Agriculture. He advanced comfortably through the ranks until, in 1959—driven by his artistic temperament—he and his wife took off for Greece so he could write a novel (*The Rise and Fall of Married Charlie*, published by Andre Deutsch). When they ran out of money they moved to England and he worked as an accounting advisor for the Oxford University Press. And then in 1969 they returned to Canada, where Tony accepted a position as Executive Director of the University of British Columbia Press in Vancouver. He remained there until he took early retirement in 1983, to pursue a personal dream to become an artist. He was successful and acquired reasonable fame as an impressionist painter working in oil and mixed media until his untimely death at age 69 in 1996, when he was at the peak of his artistic career. In his will he specified that his ashes be strewn around the De Moulpied tomb in St Martin's churchyard in Guernsey, so could return to the land of his birth.

Two of Tony's paintings are particularly significant. One is an extraordinarily insightful view of St Martin's church and the surrounding grey-granite buildings. The other is a fiery depiction of a cargo ship exploding, which he painted from memory: a disturbing reminder of what he saw from the deck of the *Batavier IV* in 1940. It hangs in the Keith Alexander Gallery in Vancouver.

Ian

Ian adapted to the Canadian way of life faster than any of us. He was nine when the evacuation took place and he subsequently entered Sir John Franklin elementary school in Winnipeg. Consequently he worked through his education years in Canada much more in step with children his own age than Tony and I had. He has the same husky voice that my father had and I have, but a much more natural Canadian accent to go with it.

On graduating from high school Ian, too, joined the Manitoba civil service in what was then the Department of Highways, and from there moved to the Department of Industry, Trade and Tourism. He became heavily involved in both industrial project development and federal-provincial government relations, and eventually was appointed Assistant Deputy Minister. After 42 years with the Province of Manitoba he elected to retire early to form his own consulting company, named Courses of Action Incorporated, providing consulting services in economic development for federal and provincial governments.

The sound early education we three brothers received in Guernsey, and latterly at Elizabeth College, stood us in good stead when we entered the workforce on graduating from grade 12. None of us had post-secondary education, yet we all achieved excellent positions in our respective fields before we retired. It's significant that we could not aspire to such promotions, or be appointed to similar positions, in today's much more academic-oriented environment. It's significant, too, that each of the three Blicq sons treated 'retirement' as an opportunity to become involved in a new phase of his career, choosing to continue working rather than 'sit back on his laurels.'

Ronald (Ron)

Just like my two brothers, I entered the Manitoba civil service on leaving school early in 1942, in my case as an audit clerk destined eventually to train as a chartered accountant. However, the war intervened and fourteen months later, on my 18th birthday, I took the first step toward achieving half of my boyhood dream (to become a 'Sparks' on a merchant ship): I joined the Royal Canadian Air Force as a trainee aircrew wireless operator. Joining the merchant marine, when one lived in the middle of the Canadian prairies thousands of miles from the nearest ocean, offered far too many obstacles!. After the war I transferred to the Royal Air Force, eventually returning to Canada to become a technical editor with an engineering firm, then a teacher of technical communication at Red River College, and now a communication consultant. But that's another story.

I tend to be a pragmatic person, which has smoothed the many transitions life has presented to me. But I have never been able to ignore the 'pull' that

Guernsey has on my emotions. The desire to return and soak up the Guernsey ambience—and remember the life I enjoyed there as a child—remains as strong as ever.

But I am not alone. Tony and Ian have both told me, at different times, that they have experienced a similar "pull," which I suppose is not to be unexpected. What has surprised me more is that our children, and our children's children who have visited Guernsey, have been similarly affected. As a ten-year-old grandson told me last year, after his first visit to the Island:

"You know, Grandpa, of all the places Mom and Dad have taken me," – and he is a reasonably travelled boy – "Guernsey is my favourite. It's…like, you know… like it's a magic place."

Wendy Cotte

After the occupation our family home had to be repaired extensively, both inside and out. The general shape and framework are the same, but the asbestos exterior walls have been replaced by white stucco and a large glass-covered sunroom has been built at the rear of the house. The new owner has completely redesigned the interior, so that my bedroom has now become the main entrance to the house. I am the only family member who has seen the internal changes: the interior now bears no resemblance to the home we once knew. I never told my parents or my brothers about these changes, preferring that they continue to remember their home as it was in the 1930s.

Endnote:

Aggression Affects *Individuals*

Television has made us instant viewers of catastrophic events, but it has lessened our sensitivity to how those affected must be feeling, particularly when the event involves a large number of people. Although we sense the horror of a major flying accident that kills 209 passengers and crew, we cannot easily come to terms with the individual tragedies that have occurred.

But when a single-passenger aeroplane experiences engine trouble and the pilot loses her life because she steers the plane out to sea rather than risk endangering the townspeople over whom she is flying, the effect is more poignant because it affects one person with whom we can more easily identify, and we can understand the grief experienced by her husband, children, and parents.

I can no longer watch masses of people escaping a war zone, as occurred in Kosovo, without realizing that *each person is an individual experiencing a personal tragedy.* The abrupt evacuation from

Guernsey, and the effect it had on each member of our family, has taught me that. Now, when I see long treks of inhabitants escaping from a war-ravaged area, I am acutely aware that each person is bearing within himself or herself the loss of security, a home, an income, a way of life, and possibly even loved ones.

An aggression occurs against *individuals*, each of whom suffers separately. We must always recognize that.

Ron Blicq
May 2, 2000